Signs of the Times

Malcolm Summers worked as a maths teacher from 1981 to 2017, and as a Deputy Head from 1993. Originally from Birmingham, he has lived in Reading for nearly 40 years. He is married with two grown up children.

By the same author

History of Greyfriars Church, Reading, Downs Way Publishing (2013)
   (Available from Greyfriars Bookshop, Reading)
Nicolas Appert, Downs Way Publishing (2015)
Henry George Willink, Downs Way Publishing (2017)

Also published by Two Rivers Press

Rural Reading by Adrian Lawson & Geoff Sawers
The Constitutionals: A work of fiction by Peter Robinson
Botanical Artistry: Plants, projects & processes by Julia Trickey
The Greenwood Trees: History, folklore and uses of Britain's trees
   by Christina Hart-Davies
Reading Abbey and the Abbey Quarter by Peter Durrant & John Painter
Reading's Bayeux Tapestry by Reading Museum
A Coming of Age: Celebrating 18 Years of Botanical Painting by the Eden Project
   Florilegium Society by Ros Franklin
Picture Palace to Penny Plunge: Reading's Cinemas by David Cliffe
The Shady Side of Town: Reading's Trees by Adrian Lawson & Geoff Sawers
Reading: The Place of the People of the Red One by Duncan Mackay
Silchester: Life on the Dig by Jenny Halstead & Michael Fulford
The Writing on the Wall by Peter Kruschwitz
Caught on Camera: Reading in the 70s by Terry Allsop
Plant Portraits by Post: Post & Go British Flora by Julia Trickey
Allen W. Seaby: Art and Nature by Martin Andrews & Robert Gillmor
Reading Detectives by Kerry Renshaw
Fox Talbot & the Reading Establishment by Martin Andrews
All Change at Reading by Adam Sowan
Cover Birds by Robert Gillmor
Caversham Court Gardens: A Heritage Guide by Friends of Caversham
   Court Gardens
Birds, Blocks & Stamps: Post & Go Birds of Britain by Robert Gillmor
Down by the River: The Thames and Kennet in Reading by Gillian Clark

Signs of the Times

Reading's Memorials

Malcolm Summers

First published in the UK in 2019 by Two Rivers Press
7 Denmark Road, Reading RG1 5PA
www.tworiverspress.com

© in text and photographs Malcolm Summers 2019

The right of the author to be identified as the author of this work
have been asserted by him in accordance with the Copyright, Designs
and Patents Act of 1988.

All rights reserved. No part of this publication may be reproduced,
stored in or introduced into a retrieval system, or transmitted,
in any form, or by any means (electronic, mechanical, photocopying,
recording or otherwise) without the prior written permission
of the publisher.

ISBN 978-1-909747-49-4

1 2 3 4 5 6 7 8 9

Two Rivers Press is represented in the UK by Inpress Ltd
and distributed by NBNi.

Cover design by Sally Castle
Text design by Nadja Guggi and typeset in Parisine

Printed and bound in Europe by Imprint Digital, Exeter

Acknowledgements

Two Rivers Press is grateful to Reading Civic Society and to Richard & Alison Bennett for supporting the publication of this book.

Reading Civic Society is pleased to support the publication of this book. Reading of today, and the future, is shaped by its past. We hope this book, which delves deeply into the town's history as revealed by its monuments and memorials, will encourage people to develop a wider understanding of Reading, and its history.

In memory of my parents

Contents

Introduction | 1

I. Vachel Almshouses Plaque 1634 | 2
II. The Compter Gate Demolished c1799 | 9
III. The Simeon Obelisk 1804 | 13
IV. Laurenthes Braag 1808 | 23
V. Joshua Vines and Forbury Hill 1831 | 29
VI. Henry West 1840 | 37
VII. Drinking Fountain 1860 | 41
VIII. The Maiwand Lion 1886 | 44
IX. Jubilee Memorial Fountain 1887 | 51
X. Queen Victoria's Statue 1887 | 57
XI. Harrinson Testimonial Cross 1887 | 63
XII. Statue of George Palmer 1891 | 69
XIII. Memorial of William Isaac Palmer 1897 | 75
XIV. Martin Hope Sutton Memorial 1902 | 81
XV. Statue of King Edward VII 1902 | 87
XVI. Dr Valpy Memorial Plaque 1904 | 93
XVII. King Henry I Memorial Cross 1909 | 99
XVIII. Goldwin Smith Plaque 1910 | 105
XIX. War Memorial 1932 | 111
XX. Spanish Civil War Memorial 1990 | 117

Afterword | 131
Bibliography | 132
Index | 135

Introduction

Reading has a long and distinguished history, although it may not be obvious at first sight. The reality, though, is that wherever you walk around the town centre you will be within a short distance of something of historical interest. The old buildings are easily spotted: the wonderfully restored Abbey ruins, of course; the three ancient parish churches of the town – Saints Mary, Laurence and Giles; the former friary church of Greyfriars; the George Hotel on King Street... Every September the list of Heritage Weekend places available to visit is impressively long.

This book tells the stories behind other, often lesser known, reminders of Reading's history, by considering some of its memorials, its plaques, statues and other monuments. Even the better known ones have secrets to yield in a retelling of their origins.

Of the many memorials in Reading's town centre I have chosen nineteen, and one more that used to be located there. Each of them can be seen as you walk along the street or in the park. They are *signs of the times*, reminding us of people and events that were felt to be of such importance that we, in the future, needed to be told lest their stories be forgotten.

I. Vachel Almshouses Plaque 1634

The almshouses in Castle Street date from 1866. They replaced five sets of earlier almshouses, including the 17th-century endowment by Sir Thomas Vachel referred to on this plaque.

Sir Thomas Vachel, or Vachell, (1560–1638) lived at Coley Park on land which had been in his family since 1309. He succeeded to the Coley estate upon the death of his uncle, also named Thomas Vachel, in 1610.[1] He was married three times. Sadly, neither his first marriage, to heiress Alice Brooke, nor his second, to Sarah Lane of Horton in Northamptonshire, lasted more than a few years. With his third wife, Lettice Knollys, daughter of Sir Francis Knollys (the younger) of Battle Manor, to whom he was married in 1616, he was blessed with a more lasting relationship, as she outlived him.[2]

On 6 January 1634 Sir Thomas gave to Reading Corporation:

> a house lately built with bricks lying in Castle streete on the south side of the said streete, the Inne called the Castle in the tenure of Edward Andrewes on the west side, and the Lane leading out of Castle streete to a Meadow called Pinckneys on the east side, and all that garden adjoining the said house and bounded in with a brick wall.[3]

This building was to be an almshouse for six 'aged and impotent [ie infirm] men, without wives.' He further funded both its upkeep and the grant of two shillings every Saturday to each of the occupants and, if there were sufficient money, a gown each and two loads of wood annually. The funding, of £40 a year, was to be received from the rent paid on various arable, meadow and pasture lands, called Great and Little Garston, in the parish of Shinfield.

The six men (four from St Mary's parish and one each from St Laurence's and St Giles's) were to be chosen by Sir Thomas in his lifetime, and thereafter by the Corporation and the owners of the Coley estate.[4] One further stipulation was that the six men were to gather both morning and evening in the central common room of the almshouse while one of them read from the Book of Common Prayer.

Although the date on the plaque (and in the chapter heading) states 1634, we would now style this date 6 January 1635. This is because at the time the year's number changed at 25 March. Dates from 1 January to 24 March therefore show what we would now consider to be the wrong year. Generally, dates are corrected to show the year change at 1 January to avoid confusion

The plaque (towards the right of the photograph) says:

> S[R] THOMAS VACHEL K[T] erected these ALMS-HOUSES
> Anno Dom. 1634, and endow'd them with Forty Pounds p. Annum
> for ever for the Maintenance of Six poor Men.

and misunderstanding. The date is corrected in John Man's *History of Reading*, although not corrected in either Coates's or Doran's *Histories*.

The original Vachel almshouses building was described, in a sale notice in 1866, as:

> All that FREEHOLD Range of Brick and Tiled Buildings known as 'Sir Thomas Vachel's Almshouses' situate on the South side of Castle Street, at the corner of Coley Street, and comprising a Dining Hall and six other Rooms, with a Yard and a Garden, having frontage of 47 feet, to Castle Street, and a depth of 91 feet 3 inches.[5]

The Vachel almshouses building was up for sale because of plans to 'consolidate' the various almshouses in Reading. The plan was to sell off the old buildings and the land in order to fund a new set of almshouses, built off Castle Street. In June 1861 a Parliament Act 'for confirming a scheme of the Charity Commissioners for certain charities in the Borough of Reading' was given Royal Assent. This created, among other changes, the Consolidated General Almshouse Charities and the Consolidated Church Almshouse Charities.

The Consolidated General Almshouse Charities included two sets of almshouses, John A'Larder's and Bernard Harrison's. In 1476 John Leche, also known as John A'Larder from his position as Steward at the Abbey, had five almshouses built in Old Street, now St Mary's Butts, and by his will in the following year added three more. Each 'almsperson' was to have a *mark* (two thirds of £1, and so 13 shillings and 4 pence) annually. These eight almshouses were rebuilt by the Corporation in 1775.[6]

Bernard Harrison, a Reading brewer, endowed his eight almshouses in 1617 in Southampton Street. These were rebuilt at the beginning of the 19th century. Each of the eight 'almswomen' received six shillings and three pence every three months.[7]

The Consolidated Church Almshouse Charities brought together three sets of almshouses, endowed by Sir Thomas Vachel, William Kendrick and John Hall.[8]

On 30 August 1634 William Kendrick, clothier of Reading, left provision for four 'almsmen' of the parishes of St Laurence and St Giles, allowing them one shilling and sixpence a week, and one 'almswoman' of St Mary's parish who received just one shilling a week. These almshouses were five tenements situated on the west side of Sieviers' Street, now Silver Street.[9]

John Hall, an apothecary, left by will dated 31 December 1696 rent on some land at Caversham to endow almshouses in Chain-lane (now Chain Street) for five poor single women, two from each of St Mary's parish and St Giles's, and one from St Laurence's. These women were to be provided with one shilling and sixpence a week, with 12 shillings a year for wood and 10 shillings for clothing.[10]

By 1861, the date of the Act to consolidate the almshouses, the various buildings were in a poor state. Those almshouses that:

were founded by Bernard Harrison, indifferent as they are, are by far the best almshouses Reading can boast; A'Larder's houses accommodate five men and three women; Harrison's eight women exclusively. These are the only almshouses in the town belonging to the General Charities, and it is well known that they are very slenderly endowed...

Kendrick's and Vachel's [almshouses] are unquestionably the worst in the town, and utterly unfit for occupation, and Hall's are inconveniently small, old, and, we should think, unhealthy. These charities are miserably endowed, and but for assistance derived from certain subsidiary 'foundations' and endowments, could not have been sustained for so long.[11]

The Charity Commissioners empowered the Trustees of the two Consolidated Charities to plan for replacing the five sets of almshouses. It allowed them to refrain from filling up any places that became available through the deaths of the 'almspeople' and so keep and invest the money that would otherwise be spent into a Building Fund. It also allowed the Trustees to sell the present almshouses and put the money gained into the fund.

The provision prior to selling off the almshouses was for the accommodation of 32 persons:

CHURCH	William Kendrick's for		4 men	1 woman
	Sir Thomas Vachel's for		6 men	
	John Hall's for			5 women
		Total	10 men	6 women
GENERAL	A' Larder's for		5 men	3 women
	Bernard Harrison's for			8 women
		Total	5 men	11 women

Therefore, the Trustees needed to create 32 almshouses to replace the old buildings. In July 1863, William H. Woodman was appointed architect for the project. The initial estimate of cost was £3,500, with each house expected to cost £100, and a further £300 for the architect's commission and incidental expenses.[12] It was thought that the sale of the old almshouses would realise about £1,500, so in March 1864 the Trustees launched an appeal to the public to raise the other £2,000. To start the process off, George Palmer pledged £400 and his brother William Isaac £100.[13] By September, the whole sum was raised.[14]

The Vachel almshouses were sold at a public auction to James Dymore Brown for £510. John Hall's almshouses in Chain Street were sold to the Trustees of the Reading Dispensary for £350. John A'Larder's almshouses sold for £300 (see Chapter XI) and William Kendrick's for £190. The Consolidated General Almshouse Charity decided to rent out Harrison's almshouses rather than to sell them.[15]

As frequently happens with building projects, the costs rose. The Trustees found that they could only afford to build 28 of the 32 almshouses, at a cost of £3,450. They committed themselves to build the remaining four almshouses as soon as their finances would allow. The new almshouses:

> will be in two continuous rows on either side of a central roadway about 35 feet wide, running from Castle-street to the Holy Brook. The houses are to be in blocks of four, half being on the ground story, and half on the floor above, with a central hall in each block, in which will be the staircase to the upper houses. Each house will have a living room about 15ft. by 10ft.; bedroom, 13ft. by 9ft.; pantry, lobby with sink, water closet, a small yard, and a coal cellar. The walls are to be of red brick with grey bands, and stone dressings to the windows and doors. There will be an ornamental stone fence between the rows of houses at the Castle-street end with iron entrance gates and ornamental stone piers. There will be a promenade ground at the end next the Holy Brook, which will be fenced off with an iron railing. A bridge will be built over the brook to a piece of garden ground on the south side of the brook.[16]

The ceremony for laying the foundation stone of the new almshouses in Castle Street took place at 2pm on Wednesday 19 April 1865. Despite poor weather, there was a very large turnout. The Mayor, Charles J. Butler, presided. Following the singing of the 100th psalm ('Make a joyful noise unto the Lord, all ye lands') led by girls from the Green School on Broad Street, the Mayor spoke of 'how the gratifying event of the day had come about'. The Town Clerk, John Jackson Blandy, read out the following document, which was placed, along with some coins of the realm, in a sealed bottle in a cavity beneath the stone:

> Borough of Reading.
> The first stone of Sixteen Almshouses for the Consolidated General Almshouse Charities of Reading, and of Twelve Almshouses for the Consolidated Church Almshouse Charities, was laid by C.J. BUTLER, ESQ., mayor, in the presence of the Trustees of the said General and Church Almshouse Charities, the Corporation of Reading and many other spectators, on Wednesday, April 19th, 1865.
>
> The names of the Trustees of the General Charities.
>
> | Rev. J. Ball | Rev. T. V. Fosbery | Chas. J. Andrewes |
> |---|---|---|
> | Chas. Ball | W. Blandy | Samuel Collier |
> | L. Cooper | W. S. Darter | W. Exall |
> | R. Hewett | R. P. Miller | J. B. Monck |
> | T. Morris | G. Palmer | H. A. Simonds |
> | T. L. Walford | | |

Church Charities.

Rev. J. Ball	Rev. T. V. Fosbery	T. F. Birch
H. B. Blandy	W. Blandy	T. Harris
W. Harris	J. Lodge	J. B. Monck
E. Morris	T. Morris	H. J. Simonds

Clerk and Solicitor of the Trustees, J. J. Blandy
Architect W. H. Woodman   Builder J. W. Sawyer

£2000 towards the cost of this work was contributed by public subscription. The residue was provided from the funds belonging to the said Almshouse Charities.

The Mayor then used a silver trowel to spread the mortar on the foundation stone, going 'through the usual formula with plumb and mallet,' and so the stone was laid. The Rev A. P. Cust (Vicar of St Mary's Church) then prayed, and the ceremony was over. There followed a dinner at the Town Hall for almost 60 gentlemen, with many speeches and much congratulation all round.[17]

The almshouses were completed by early 1866, and the men and women who were living in the old accommodation were transferred to the new. The Consolidated Charities advertised in March 1866 for candidates to apply to fill the remaining places, nine for men and five for women, with the election to take place on 13 April 1866, almost exactly a year from the laying of the foundation stone.[18] The last four almshouses (on the eastern side, next to the Holy Brook) were built in 1870 at a cost of just under £600.[19]

In 1958 the two Consolidated Charities became one by Act of Parliament, and the almshouses became governed by Reading General Municipal Charities. In turn, this has been replaced by the Reading Almshouse Charity.[20]

The original Vachel almshouses plaque from 1634 was rediscovered in July 1954. A workman who was stripping cement from a wall of the United Yeast Company's building in Castle Street found the plaque fixed into the wall.[21] The Director of Reading Museum, W. A. Smallcombe, thought that since the plaque was much older than the wall it was cemented into, it had probably been put there in order to preserve it.

Eight years later the plaque was affixed to the wall of the first block of houses on the west side following the refurbishment and modernisation of the almshouses in 1960-1962. This has led some to believe that the almshouses are just Vachel almshouses, and not, as we have seen, a consolidation of the five sets of almshouses in Reading in the middle of the 19th century.

The Vachel plaque is accompanied by two other plaques, the first of which incorrectly ascribes the buildings to 1867, rather than 1865-6:

The top plaque says:

> THESE ALMSHOUSES BUILT IN 1867 PARTLY BY PUBLIC SUBSCRIPTION
> AND PARTLY BY FUNDS OF THE MUNICIPAL CHARITIES
> WERE MODERNISED IN 1960-1962

The bottom plaque says:

> THIS PLAQUE WAS FIXED ON SIR THOMAS VACHEL'S ALMSHOUSES
> NOW KNOWN AS 67 CASTLE STREET AND WAS REMOVED
> WHEN THOSE ALMSHOUSES WERE DEMOLISHED.
> THE PROCEEDS OF THE SALE OF THAT PROPERTY
> HELPED TO BUILD THESE ALMSHOUSES.
> THIS PLAQUE WAS RE-FIXED HERE IN 1962

67 Castle Street, mentioned on the bottom plaque, no longer exists as it was removed (as was Coley Street) by the Inner Distribution Road works in the 1970s.

The almshouses are now Grade II Listed buildings, albeit under the incorrect name of 'Vachel Almshouses'. The listing description, which misunderstands the plaques because of not knowing the history behind them, is:

> Founded by Sir Thomas Vachel in 1634 and then moved to this site. See plaques. Rebuilt 1864–67, architect William Henry Woodman. 2 storey cottages in 2 reflecting rows, stepped down to Holy Brook in groups of 4. Vernacular style. Red brick with grey brick bands and decoration and with stone dressings. Tiled roofs with crested ridges; red brick ridge chimneys with grey decoration and cogged bands.
>
> Nos 5 to 16 and 21 to 32: 5 windows, 2 being canted dormered bays flanking central entrance and 2 light windows with chamfered mullions. Pointed doorways with shouldered lintels and tumbled brick in arches, strap hinges.
>
> Nos 1 to 4 and 17 to 20: also 5 bays but in 3 staggered planes. 1st plane has corbelled 1st floor window to street and a bay to front. 2nd plane now has tower porch with encorbelled parapet, pointed entrance and trefoil headed side window. This part formerly (till 1957) had a turret over. 3rd plane has gabled bay. Low screen wall to street with cast and wrought iron rails and gates.[22]

The almshouses' accommodation now consists of 26 flats, of which four are two-bedroom and the remainder one-bedroom. To qualify as a resident, a person must be of good character; be in need; and have resided within 20 miles of St Mary's Church for at least three years at some stage in their life, with preference given to those aged over 55 years.[23]

II. The Compter Gate Demolished c1799

The West or Compter Gate was the main Abbey entrance and exit, communicating directly with the town. In the late 18th century the gate was demolished because its condition had deteriorated. A small plaque on the south wall of St Laurence's Church marks the location of the gate.

The 12th-century Abbey was built on a magnificent scale. Its grounds were extensive, covering approximately 30 acres, bounded by a wall with four gateways set into it, and by the Holy Brook and the River Kennet to the south. The North, or River, Gate gave access towards the meadows by the Thames. If it were still standing it would be on the roundabout where Forbury Road meets Vastern Road, near the north-west entrance to the Forbury Gardens.

Working clockwise around the perimeter, the long Plummery Wall stretched along the north side of the Forbury Road, becoming the west side as it turned towards the Kennet. The East Gate opened onto what is now Blake's Bridge and the road to London. The River Kennet formed the next part of the boundary and then the Holy Brook with various Abbey buildings close to, or in the case of the Mill, over the Brook. In the south-west corner of the grounds stood the South Gate, near where Abbey Square meets King's Road, just across from the entrance to the Central Library.

The abbey wall turned north at this point towards St Laurence's Church, where the West, or Compter, Gate stood. Just beyond St Laurence's was the Abbey Guest House, the Hospitium. Originally St Laurence's Church was only about half its present length and lay entirely outside the Abbey walls. The Compter Gate was then at its east end. In 1196 Abbot Hugh II rebuilt and extended the Hospitium and at the same time extended the church into Abbey lands and attached it to the Hospitium as an endowment.[24] Thereafter the Compter Gate met the south wall of St Laurence's at about the middle of its length – the location now being shown, of course, by the plaque.

A 'Compter', or sometimes Counter, was a prison, and the Compter Gate was so called as it had, above the arch of the Gate, three rooms for 'any criminals belonging to the town, as well as any monks who had been guilty of insubordination.'[25] Next to the Gate was a porter's lodge. This accommodation was described, in a survey taken at the end of the Civil War, in some detail:

> The porter's lodge at the West gate entering into the said Forbury, consisting of a cellar, a hall, a buttery, three chambers, three garrets, a small yard and garden with an outhouse, in the occupation of William Newton, bounded with the Forbury, to north, and butting upon a prison called the compter, to west...[26]

The Compter Gate led into the open area of the Forbury, and by a road straight ahead to the west doors of the Abbey Church. Along this road was the Inner Gate, which of course still stands, although much altered over time. This gateway led into the area reserved for the monks, with the abbot's lodge,

cloisters, refectory, dormitory and other buildings clustered mainly to the south of the Abbey Church.

The Compter Gate was always a busy thoroughfare, both during the 418 years that the Abbey flourished, and afterwards until the Gate's demolition 260 years later. Royalty passed through the Gate many times, not only during the Abbey's life but also afterwards as the Abbey and its lands passed into the King's possession at the dissolution, becoming a royal palace until Elizabeth's reign. Thereafter, by the charter that Elizabeth gave the town, the Compter Gate and prison became the property of the Corporation.[27]

In 1619, with £100 bequeathed by the mathematician John Blagrave (c1561–1611), a six-arched covered arcade was built onto the south side of St Laurence's Church to the west of the Compter Gate. The arcade was called Blagrave's Piazza and was also generally known as 'Church Walk.' As well as being a walkway, the Piazza was used by the Town Council to store the stocks and the pillory used in the nearby Market Place. In the arch closest to the Compter Gate, a single prison cell was built, known as the 'Hole', which was used to detain anyone apprehended at night.

In 1636, Sir Francis Knollys gained the agreement of both the Church authorities and Reading Corporation to extend the church into the gap between the Piazza and the Compter Gate. *Reading Records* states:

> At this daye the Mayour and Burgesses graunted and confirmed the void plot of ground adjoining to St Lawrence's Churche, between the Counter [ie Compter] Wall and the Walke [ie the Piazza], to Sir Frauncis Knollis th'elder, and his heires, to th'intent that at his own charges he shall build an Isle thereupon to be and remayne to the Churche for ever.[28]

By the following year, the Knollys' Transept or Aisle was built both to seat his family in the church and to create a burial place beneath. This structure was removed in January 1868 although the remains of the Knollys family were not removed from beneath it, so the pavement covers the many graves.[29]

The Compter prison served to incarcerate people for a wide variety of crimes. Here are a few examples from the 1630s:

Rose Underwood – for stealing and then attempting to sell pewter plates
John Scott – for forsaking his wife and children
Elizabeth Hill – for vagrancy
John Hasteed – for suspected theft of a horse
William Lawley – for suspected rape[30]

The Compter prison came to be used predominantly as a debtors' prison. By the late 18th century the house on the corner of Market Place, next to the Gate and opposite St Laurence's Church, was known as the Compter House.

Plaque on the south wall of St Laurence's Church

This was used both as the Magistrate's Court (until 1862 when the Magistrates moved to Highbridge House)[31] and as the abode of one of the town's Sergeants of police. When the prison reformer John Howard visited the Compter, now doubling up as a public house, he noted:

> Reading Town Gaol or Compter:
>
> Three rooms in a public house (the Reading arms) belonging to the town. The eldest serjeant has generally the refusal of it. No court. No water. Felon's allowance three pence a day. Keeper no salary.: fees 4s. 4d., no table. 1776 November 1st Debtors – 2
>
> 1779 April 21st No prisoners[32]

In 1796 Mr Simeon[33] applied to the Reading Corporation asking them to brick up one of the Compter prison windows, on the east, as it overlooked his yard. The Corporation agreed to block that window and subsequently opened another one to the north that would not be intrusive to their neighbour.[34]

By September 1799 the Corporation had decided that they must replace the 'Old Compter and Prison'.[35] Somewhere around this time the old Gate was demolished, but unfortunately its passing does not seem to have been noted either in the local press or in the annals of the Corporation.

III. The Simeon Obelisk 1804

This unusual monument in Market Place was erected in late July/early August 1804. It commemorates Edward Simeon, a native of the town, who gave the money for the obelisk and for it to be perpetually lit at the same times as the recently installed town lighting.[36]

Edward Simeon was born in 1758, the third son of Richard and Elizabeth Simeon of the Forbury, Reading. Edward's eldest brother died at a young age. The second brother was John, later Sir John Simeon, 1st Baronet of Wallinscot, who was one of Reading's two MPs from 1797 to 1802 and again from 1806 to 1818. John also held the office of Recorder of Reading from 1779 until 1807. Edward's younger brother, Charles, became a leading Evangelical clergyman, ministering in Holy Trinity Church in Cambridge from age 24 until he died aged 77 in 1836.

Edward was 'an eminent merchant in London and for many years one of the Directors of the Bank of England'.[37] He amassed a large fortune and became well known for his generosity. In giving notice of his death on 7 December 1812, one newspaper wrote: 'On Monday last, at Salvador House, Bishopsgate-street, London, Edward Simeon, Esq. brother of John Simeon Esq. M.P. for Reading. The virtue and benevolence of his nature displayed in the most extensive charities will render his death a severe affliction to the unfortunate, and secure for his memory that unfeigned respect which attended him in public and private life.'[38]

In spite of living and working in London, Edward Simeon never forgot his native town. Each year, for example, he paid for new clothes for all the children attending the Sunday Schools in the three parishes of Reading, as well as in all the dissenting congregations, leaving a legacy of £2,500 in trust to the Corporation to continue thereafter.[39] John Man, in his 1816 *History of Reading*, wrote:

> While speaking of the charities which do credit to the donors, we must add the very generous donations for which the poor of the present day are indebted to the philanthropy of E. Simeon, esq. who has done more for the benefit of the poor than they ever experienced from any former benefactor. In the winter season, since the year 1802, till his death, this gentleman has been in the habit of distributing among poor families, blankets, and under-garments for the women, besides clothing a number of children of both sexes, in neat dresses befitting their situation in life; and every year on the election of a new mayor, they, together with the school charity children, were paraded in the market-place, and regaled with a large plumb-cake: this, though it may appear a trifling circumstance in the eyes of some, is a higher gratification to the infant mind than even their new dress, whereby they appear elevated above their equals.[40]

On 24 January 1804, Edward Simeon wrote to the Mayor, Mr Lancelot Austwick, and Corporation of Reading:

My Dear Sir,

It has very often struck me that the want of light in so great and public a spot as the Market Place was productive of Inconvenience which every Inhabitant and Neighbour must experience. I have frequently felt a secret wish to remedy the Inconvenience, at the same time I have had my Doubts as to the proper mode of gratifying this feeling.

At length I have resolved to address you, Sir, on the subject, and request that you will make known my wish of erecting at my own expence an obelisk in the center of the Market Place – protected with Iron Railing and Spurs or Curb Stones to resist the heaviest shock of a Waggon – The obelisk to have four Lamps.

And it is my further wish to invest in the public Funds in the name of the Mayor and Corporation such a Sum as will defray forever the Expence of lighting the same during the period when the other public Lamps are lighted.

I beg to add that the Erection will contribute essentially to prevent the confusion which now prevails with the Waggons on Market days, by obliging the Drivers to take a regular line. The moment you are so good as to convey to me the acquiescence of the Corporation, the architect will be directed to present the proposed plan for their consideration & carry the same into immediate effect – your respectable body having at all times manifested the strongest desire to promote any Improvement in the Town, will I trust on this occasion, Honor me with their co-operation. I beg to subscribe myself with great esteem,

Yours most faithfully
Edward Simeon[41]

The letter was read at a meeting of the Corporation a week later and received a very positive response, with the Mayor and six aldermen being nominated as a committee to receive Simeon's plan and attend to it on behalf of the Corporation.[42]

Simeon engaged as architect for the project John (later Sir John) Soane, who had from 1788 been architect to the Bank of England where Simeon was a director (1792–1811). Like Simeon, Soane had Reading connections. He was born in 1753, probably in Goring, and was educated in William Baker's school in Reading.[43] Prior to this commission, Soane had already worked in Reading,

Simeon Obelisk in Market Place with the Corn Exchange entrance behind and to the left

having designed a house and brewery for Mr William Blackall Simonds, head of H. & G. Simonds Brewery, in 1790. Soane also created three designs for a new house for Lancelot Austwick in the mid-1790s, none of which were actually used for Austwick's new house in Friar Street, built in 1808. It is often thought that this house, which later became the Greyfriars Vicarage, was designed by Soane, but it was not.[44] The house was demolished in 1963.

Soane sent drawings of his proposal to Simeon on 4 April 1804, with a copy to the Mayor (presumably after Simeon had given his agreement) on 27 April.[45] The Soane Museum has a small mahogany model of the obelisk crafted at the time, which can be viewed online.[46] This model probably accompanied the drawings so that the design could be better visualised.

At a meeting of the Corporation on 15 May 1804, the committee reported back that 'a plan of an intended obelisk or building as an ornament as well as improvement of the Market Place by lighting the same was produced agreeable to Mr Edward Simeon's proposal of the 31st January last... [The] proposal was agreed to and ... was signed by the Mayor, who was requested to communicate the same to Mr Edwd Simeon.'[47]

Soane had produced an unusual design – seemingly a triangular-based obelisk, but in fact hexagonal with alternate short and long faces. Obelisks are generally four-sided, whether square or rectangular based. It is not certain why this one is triangular, but it has been suggested that it is to reflect the shape of the Market Place around it.

Soane produced final drawings, dated 29 May 1804, and was in Reading to supervise the beginning of the construction of the obelisk 19–21 July. The obelisk was sculpted in Portland stone by Robert Spiller, who had worked for Soane previously, and who was paid £310.3s.[48]

The three faces each have a brass plaque. On the south face, the one farthest from St Laurence's Church and facing into the Market Place, the plaque states:

ERECTED
AND LIGHTED FOREVER,
AT THE EXPENCE OF
EDWARD SIMEON ESQ^r
AS A MARK OF AFFECTION
TO HIS NATIVE TOWN
AD 1804.
LANCELOT AUSTWICK ESQ^r.
MAYOR

On the other two faces are the shields of the Borough and of Edward Simeon. The base of the obelisk has three rounded piers to support the lanterns, each pier decorated with a carving of *fasces* – a bundle of rods with an axe in the middle – symbolising strength through unity. Five vertical flutes adorn each of the three main upper faces of the obelisk, with a fret design on the narrower edges. Above is a hemisphere that has been cut vertically, parallel to the faces, with a cylinder capped by an acorn (or possibly a pineapple – opinions differ!)

Although the *Reading Mercury* made no mention of any ceremony or unveiling, it could have been on Monday 3 September 1804, since John Soane noted that he surveyed the monument that day.[49] The obelisk soon appeared in the newspapers, though, in a report of a 'Venison Dinner' hosted by Reading's Whig MP, Charles Shaw Lefevre, for 400 at the Town Hall on Thursday 6 September. In one of the after-dinner speeches in support of Mr Lefevre, Mr John Berkeley Monck referred to it. The newspaper reported:

> Several other gentlemen, on their healths being drank, delivered their sentiments, and alluded particularly to the means that had been resorted to by the adversaries of our worthy Member to influence many worthy electors, and were very strenuous and successful in the exposure of them. Mr Monck was remarkably happy in his allusion to a certain newly erected monument, by observing that some gentlemen endeavoured to ingratiate themselves with the Electors, by raising monuments of stone, and having their transitory names emblazoned on them in brass, but his friend had raised a more lasting monument in the breasts and hearts of his constituents.[50]

Edward Simeon's motives for erecting the obelisk and its lanterns were thus called into question from the first: altruism and desire to serve his native town? Or publicity for the family name and so in support of his brother John, a Tory, who had lost his seat at Westminster in 1802 and would soon no doubt be contesting it again? (Indeed, John did win back one of Reading's two seats at the next election in 1806.) Whatever the truth of his motives, there is no doubting Edward's generosity. Within a few days he wrote:

> BROTHER TOWNSMEN,
>
> Having received many anonymous Letters, stating the extreme want of Dwellings for the poor Inhabitants of this Borough, and inviting me to come to their relief;
>
> I beg to answer them, by saying, that I will, with the greatest pleasure, subscribe ONE THOUSAND POUNDS, towards the Building of Houses for their Accommodation; and as Timber is the most costly Article in such a Plan, I will further undertake to procure it at the lowest importation price.
>
> The increased Affection which I daily observe towards me, excites in my heart the desire of furthering your Wishes.
>
> Reading, Sept. 11, 1804
> EDWARD SIMEON[51]

The report of the Town Hall dinner was followed by a run of correspondence in the *Reading Mercury* between 'An Elector' (supporting John Simeon) and 'A Real Elector' (supporting Mr Lefevre). The obelisk became a part of this attempt to score political points off one another.

'An Elector' wrote to challenge the article's accuracy, and regarding the obelisk said: As to Mr Monck's speech, referring to the Column, it was scarcely touched upon when an almost general hiss marked the wounded feelings of the company, which turned his intended invective into a flowery compliment to Mr Lefevre. This incident has been carefully suppressed.'[52]

In reply the following week, 'A Real Elector' resorted to using more insulting language, stating that Simeon was attempting to 'bias the heads of the Borough in his favour by setting up in the market place a *paltry geegaw thing* without use, or name.' There is a footnote at this point that is more insulting: 'The writer to whom this is addressed calls it a column:– perhaps of some new order in architecture for I never met with a three cornered column among the old ones. Some denominate it an obelisk, others a pillar, but among the generality of the inhabitants, it is called a p****** post.'[53] [Emphasis and asterisks as in the original.]

The final volley against Edward Simeon and the obelisk came again from 'A Real Elector,' who claimed that there had been no explanation from Mr Simeon as to:

> why he has opened a warehouse to supply the town with merchandise *without the middle-man's profit*, to the great loss of wholesale dealers? Nor why the *Pretty Dears* of Reading were taken to the races in Mr Simeon's carriage, and treated with a new invented *little go*? Nor why Mr E. Simeon imported a cargo of *thimbles* to be fitted on the fingers of the fair with his own hands, nor, lastly, why the eighth wonder of the world, *a three-cornered column*, was erected in the Market-place —
>
> 'On a spruce pedestal of Wedgewood ware,
> 'Where *motley arms* and tawdry *emblems glare*.'[54]

The obelisk was encircled by iron railings and a set of nine bollards, three to each side, to protect it.[55] However, the lights had not yet been installed. In January 1805 the following letter from Edward Simeon was read at the Corporation meeting:

Dear Sir,

The Corporation did me the honor some time since of accepting my proposition to erect an Obelisk in the Market Place, and of embellishing the same with Lamps, as a small token of my affection to my Native Town. The Corporation also did me the honor to accept of a Fund for the purpose of defraying the expence of lighting the same for ever. This building has since been carried into effect, and I trust meets your approbation, as being both useful and Ornamental, and free from the objection of occasioning the smallest hindrance to the Market.

A variety of Experiments have been made in order to produce the most effectual and brilliant light, and at length the preference has been given to burners containing two tiers of lights, three above and four below, each burner containing thirty-six threads of cotton, so that the three lamps are to give a light equal to twenty-seven of the Town Lamps, as is more fully explained in the annexed Contract with Mr Thomas Owen who lights the Town Lamps.

The agreement in the first instance was made for a still larger body of light, but the Surveyor and Contractor both thought it superfluous. I wish to reserve to myself however the liberty of increasing the body of light if at any future period it should be thought necessary.

The annual charge of Mr Thomas Owen for cleansing and lighting these Lamps is £22.5s.6d.

To meet this and any other incidental Charge, I have the honor to enclose the Bank Receipt for the sum of £1000 – 3 p^{r}c^t reduced, transferred in the names of the Mayor and Corporation of the Borough of Reading.

I beg Sir you will do me the favor to assure the Corporation collectively and individually that it is the summit of my ambition to merit their esteem and regard.

I have yet a request to make Sir of you and the Gentlemen of the Corporation; which is, that you will have the goodness to apply the enclosed Bank Note of £100 to assist the industrious and helpless poor in the three Parishes of Reading, at this inclement season when work runs short; by furnishing them with bread, six pence under the price of the quartern loaf, in the following manner – each member of the Corporation to distribute Tickets for 150 loaves – and you Sir to distribute Tickets for 400 – to such poor objects as you think proper and to avoid a preference to any particular Baker (there being twenty five in the Town) I will thank you each to select one.

Believe me with regard
Dear Sir
Yours most sincerely
Edward Simeon [56]

In response the Council publicly declared:

At a Common Hall of the Corporation holden in the Guildhall of this Borough on Friday the 11th day of January 1805 a letter from Edward Simeon Esq. dated January the 7th 1805 addressed to the Worshipful

> the Mayor was read stating that he had transferred to the Mayor and Corporation 1000£ 3 per cent reduced annuities as a perpetual fund for lighting the Lamps affixed to the obelisk lately erected by him in the Market Place; and also conveying to the Mayor a Bank Note of 100£ to assist the industrious and helpless poor of the three Parishes of Reading at this inclement season.
>
> After which it was unanimously resolved that the thanks of this Hall be given to Edward Simeon Esq. not only for erecting this said obelisk and his munificent endowment thereof but for his liberal present to the Poor, and as a further testimony of the sense entertained by the Corporation of his constant attention and kindness to this his native Town –
>
> It was also unanimously resolved and ordered that Edward Simeon Esq. be presented with the Freedom of this Borough.[57]

The gift of £1,000 '3 per cent reduced annuities' became therefore a charitable gift that the Corporation administered. In W. E. M. Blandy's *History of the Reading Municipal Charities*, he notes that:

> This Stock was transferred in 1883 into the name of the Official Trustee; the dividends were used in paying for the gas supplied to the three lamps on the obelisk, and a grant of £5 to the Corporation towards the illumination of the clock on the tower of the passage to the Corn Exchange. The surplus income was used from time to time in keeping the whole structure of the Obelisk and rails in repair...
>
> In 1911 the Trustees were anxious to utilise part of the income of the Charity for the payment of pensions to the inmates of the Almshouses, but the Charity Commissioners declined to sanction the project. About this time, the gas lamps at the Obelisk were discontinued and eventually, in 1912, the Charity Commissioners made an order allowing the Trustees to pay £20 a year to the Queen Victoria Institute for nursing the sick poor of Reading. Subject to this payment the balance of income was to be accumulated and used for the repair of the Obelisk.
>
> In 1948, the Queen Victoria Institute was taken over by the State under the National Health Insurance Act 1947, and the payments were discontinued. Since then, the income has been accumulated in a repair fund which at the moment [1968] shows a considerable balance.[58]

In 1810 *The Stranger in Reading*, purporting to be an account by a visitor in a series of letters to a friend but actually by the Reading publisher John Man, was highly critical of much of the town. Of the obelisk, he wrote in a puzzled vein that he could not distinguish the style of architecture of this 'large stone lamp post', as it featured British, Roman and Egyptian features. He summed it up by saying: 'It is surrounded by a handsome iron railing, and may, upon the whole, be called a pretty, rather than a correct, design for a lamp post.'[59] Man added that if the 'lamp post' had rather been a fountain, then that would have served the people of Reading better. About twenty years later a public water pump was added on the south side of the obelisk, close to the railing.[60]

The 'Simeon Monument' is a Grade II* Listed building, signifying that it is a building of 'more than special interest.' The current listing details state:

> Designed by Sir John Soane. Portland stone fluted obelisk with chamfered sides (key pattern) which have palmette tympana cut into capping. Striated cylinder over capped by pineapple. Rusticated triangular base with lobed corners, each with fasces in relief and with bracketed cast and wrought iron lamp overthrows. Moulded panels on each face – bronze tablet to south inscribed: 'Erected and lighted forever at the expense of Edward Simeon Esqre, as a mark of affection to his native town AD1804. Lancelot Austwick Esq Mayor'. Contemporary railings, cast iron with fleur de lys heads and heavy standards.[61]

The obelisk, and the surrounding area, have gone through many alterations over the last 200 years.[62] In 2007 it was cleaned and restored by Bedford Road stone masons A. F. Jones as part of Reading Borough Council's modernisation of Market Place.[63] It now stands at the centre of an open pedestrian area, with flower baskets beneath its lamps and surrounded by bench seating.

IV. Laurenthes Braag 1808

A memorial tablet on the exterior of St Mary's Church remembers a Danish merchant who died aged 25 in September 1808 when he was a prisoner of war on parole in Reading.

Laurenthes (also known by the Latinised version Lorentius) Braag was born on 21 July 1783 on the island of St Croix, which had been part of the Danish West Indies for 50 years. His parents, Paul Braag and Christiane Moller, had been married at the St Croix Lutheran Church in early 1782. Paul, a weigh-master by royal appointment, died about a year after his son Laurenthes was born. Records next show Laurenthes when he was aged 4 in the care of Dominicus and Cecilia Braag, probably his father's brother and wife. Dominicus was also a weigh-master, at St Croix's main port of Christiansted. It looks likely that they brought Laurenthes up as their own son.

After his uncle's death in Christiansted in 1796, his aunt moved to Copenhagen and remarried. By this time Laurenthes was aged 13 and soon his thoughts turned to seeking his fortune by going to sea.[64]

This was a time of war and disruption throughout Europe. The French Revolutionary Wars began in 1792, becoming in due course the Napoleonic Wars, and embroiled Denmark in spite of the country's best efforts to remain neutral. Napoleon aimed to force Denmark into alliance and use their navy to invade England. The French mustered their troops for an invasion of Denmark from the south. England could not take the risk that the Danish fleet might fall into enemy hands and so gave Denmark an ultimatum. Denmark was to choose from three options: ally with England; hand its fleet over to England for safe-keeping for the duration of the war as a pledge of their neutrality; or be considered an enemy. England did not get any response to its ultimatum and so invaded Denmark, bombarding Copenhagen in September 1807. Denmark lost much of its fleet and was forced into alliance with Napoleon.

Throughout these years both sides in the conflict took thousands of prisoners of war. When an English ship captured any enemy vessels, whether navy or merchant, any survivors were brought back to port and handed over to the Admiralty Transport Office. Common seamen were imprisoned on prison 'hulks' – old ships made unseaworthy by the removal of masts. Those considered to be officers and gentlemen were usually put on 'parole.' This meant that they could live in a community under a curfew with their movements being restricted to within a given area.

Reading was host to several hundred prisoners of war on parole, especially in the period 1807 to 1814. Although several nationalities are mentioned in various sources, the Danish prisoners made up by far the majority and had the

Memorial Tablet on the outside of the south wall St Mary's Church

greatest effect on their host town. The town's first experience of prisoners of war, however, seems to have been large groups of French prisoners being moved through the town to other locations. First 300 and then 600 passed through in October 1800, and a further 500 in 1806.[65] The first Danish prisoners of war in Reading were a group of 32 who arrived in the town on 14 November 1807. By the end of that month a total of 173 Danish prisoners had arrived and were lodged in Reading.[66]

Laurenthes Braag was captured from the Merchant Vessel *Harriett* in the very early days of the conflict with England, on 24 July 1807.[67] He was brought to Dover and by 28 November was on parole in Reading. In the Admiralty Register at Dover, Laurenthes' description was given as:

Age 24	height 5 feet 8 inches	light hair
grey eyes	fair complexion	round face
stout person	no visible marks or wounds[68]	

At their destination, prisoners on parole were met and lodged by the local 'Agent' on behalf of the Admiralty Transport Office. In Reading, the Agent was Mr Herbert Lewis, later Alderman Lewis, who gained the reputation of dealing with the prisoners with sympathy and interest.

On the whole, the people of Reading seemed to take these Danish prisoners of war to their hearts, even though the situation probably led to overcrowding in the town. In addition to many prisoners of war, people were arriving from coastal regions, fleeing inland from the expected invasion. In a contemporary diary, published seventy years later, the diarist wrote, after Napoleon was defeated and sent to Elba:

> It was predicted that when peace came Reading would revert to her original size; that there being no longer any fear of invasion, the people would resort to the seashore and leave many houses without inhabitant; but, instead of this [houses] are still [being erected] and occupied as soon as they are finished.[69]

Within a month of Laurenthes' arrival, some Danish prisoners were freed. The *Reading Mercury* reported: 'This day, 19 of the Danish prisoners on parole here, left this town, ... returning to Denmark; they being included in the capitulation of Gen. Peyman, which provided that the prisoners of each side, made before that time, should be restored.'[70] This referred to the capitulation on 6 September 1807 of Copenhagen, where General Peyman was Governor. The *Articles of Capitulation* stated: 'Article VIII. All Prisoners taken on both sides, shall be unconditionally restored; and those officers who are prisoners on parole, shall be released from its effects.'[71] It is not known why Laurenthes Braag, who had been captured 'before that time', was not one of those 'unconditionally restored'.

While on parole, in the years 1807 to 1814, eight Danish prisoners died and were buried in one of the three parishes of Reading:

Laurenthes Braag
Captured 24 July 1807 from Merchant Vessel *Harriett*
Age 24, Merchant
Died 3 September 1808
Buried 6 September 1808 St Mary's

Markus Brandt
Captured from Merchant Vessel *Triton*
Died 7 March 1809
Buried 10 March 1809 St Laurence's

Conrad Ament
Captured 10 December 1807 from Merchant Vessel *Montreal*
Age 40
Died 1 June 1809
Buried 5 June 1809 St Laurence's

Hans Jurgen Lemeke
Captured 5 April 1808 from Merchant Vessel *Amuita*
Master of Vessel
Died 14 August 1809
Buried 17 August 1809 St Laurence's

Knud Fredericksen
Captured 14 November 1808 from Merchant Vessel *No. 20*
Master of Vessel
Died 7 September 1810
Buried 10 September 1810 St Mary's

Erick Halversen
Captured 3 November 1809 from Merchant Vessel *St Maria*
Age 50, Master of Vessel
Died 19 March 1812
Buried 23 March 1812 St Laurence's

Torvel Johnsen
Captured 7 September 1811 from Merchant Vessel *Lykkens Haab*
Age 30, Mate
Buried 21 January 1814 St Laurence's

Anthony Jorgensen
Captured 7 May 1812 from Merchant Vessel *Anna Maria Catherina*
Age 26, Mate
Died 30 April 1814
Buried 3 May 1814 St Giles[72]

The first to die was Laurenthes Braag, on 3 September 1808, aged 25. It is not known what he died of. Perhaps it was because he was the first that his Danish and Reading friends subscribed to erect a memorial tablet. Or he may simply have been a popular figure in the community who would be sorely missed. His funeral was held on Wednesday 6 September at St Mary's Church.[73] Following Laurenthes' death his effects were sold and Mr Lewis, as Agent, was credited with the amount raised: £21 13s 1d. This would then have been committed to the common purse to support the Danish prisoners, whose allowance was not generous.

The people of Reading showed their kindness to the Danish prisoners by contributing to their funds to enable them to have a reasonable standard of living. In September 1808, for example, soon after Laurenthes died, Mr Lewis advertised in the *Reading Mercury*:

> The Danish Prisoners of War, on parole at Reading, beg to return their grateful acknowledgements to those ladies and gentlemen who have kindly contributed to their subscription fund, as well as to the inhabitants in general, for the hospitality manifested towards them; they take the liberty of stating that this fund, from which they have hitherto received an allowance of 2s. 6d. each per week, is now quite exhausted; and as their friends in their native country are prohibited, under pain of death, from holding any communication with them, in their present unfortunate situation they are induced once more to appeal to the known generosity of the British Public. A further subscription for their relief is already begun by some merchants and gentlemen in London, which they humbly hope will be extended to this town, and neighbourhood, more especially as the winter season is now approaching, when their wants will be necessarily increased. Subscriptions will be thankfully received at either of the Banking Houses, in this and the adjacent towns, or by Mr H. Lewis, Agent, for Prisoners of War. And the names of Subscribers will be published in a future paper unless otherwise desired.[74]

In response, in just over a month £163 was donated, including a donation of 10 guineas from the Woodley Volunteer Troop of Cavalry.[75]

Each month brought more Danish prisoners to Reading, sometimes fewer than 10, but occasionally many more – 68 in July 1808, for example. As well as the occasional prisoner receiving their freedom – usually when a prisoner exchange had been agreed – numbers decreased due to escapes. Leaving Reading was not difficult but managing to take ship and leave the shores would have been trickier. This did not stop the 83 who, over the seven years, broke their parole and left, although whether many reached home is not known.[76]

On 25 October 1809, at the celebration of the Golden Jubilee of King George III, a general amnesty was proclaimed and the Danish prisoners – almost 200 in Reading – were set free. The Danes, by way of thanks to the town for its hospitality and kind treatment, presented the Mayor and Corporation with a model ship of war, made by one of their number, Sivert Riiberg. This model now resides in Reading Museum.[77]

It was only two months before the next group of Danish prisoners arrived, with nine transferred from Chatham just before Christmas. However, while almost 500 Danish prisoners had been on parole in Reading between November 1807 and October 1809, with usually over 250 prisoners in the town at any one time, there were just 49 between December 1809 and 1811. Unfortunately, no records for the final three years of captivity to 1814 have been found.[78]

As well as the Danish and French prisoners, there were 'about 150 Dutch officers, who have been here some time on their parole of honour', having been captured at the Isle of Java. They were released in December 1813.[79] In 1815, there were also some German prisoners in the town.[80]

In May 1814, prisoners from Norway on parole in Reading sent Mr J. B. Monck a letter of thanks for a speech he made decrying the English blockade of their country. Their letter acknowledged 'the regard he and the people in general entertain'd for their welfare'.[81]

Sources also mention American prisoners. The diarist of *Reading Seventy Years Ago* states in the entry for 27 June 1814: 'The Americans, prisoners in this town, were removed to Devonshire because they did not behave properly.'[82] The Americans' behaviour is in marked contrast to that of the Danes, who became known in Reading as 'The Gentlemen Danes', according to the memoir by Hans Birch Dahlerup, a Danish Lieutenant and one of the prisoners on parole in Reading, cited in John Nixon's *The Gentlemen Danes*.[83]

At the general peace that was signalled by the Treaty of Fontainebleau in April 1814, all the remaining prisoners were allowed home. Some, however, chose to stay. On 11 June 1814, Hans Poulsen (a Seaman volunteer) married Sarah Binfield at St Laurence's Church. Poulsen had been captured in October 1808 and would have been freed in the general amnesty on 25 October 1809, so must have chosen to remain in Reading thereafter. Then on 16 June 1814, Lt Hans Bodenheffs married architect's daughter Sarah Selina Cooper at St Giles.[84]

The only Danish prisoner other than Laurenthes Braag to be buried at St Mary's Church was Knud Fredericksen. A memorial tablet was erected on the exterior of the south wall of the church, but this is now lost. It can be seen, for example, in a photograph taken by Fox Talbot, which shows St Mary's before its restoration in 1860.[85]

Although happily not lost, the memorial tablet to Laurenthes Braag gradually deteriorated and by the early part of this century it was barely legible. The Reading Civic Society raised the £1,300 needed to restore it. Then on 29 October 2009 Canon Brian Shenton of St Mary's led a service to rededicate the memorial. The service was attended by one of Laurenthes' relatives, Birgith Braag Winther, and many dignitaries, including the Mayor of Reading, Councillor Fred Pugh. A military re-enactment group mounted a guard, dressed in red uniforms of the Napoleonic period.[86]

V. Joshua Vines and Forbury Hill 1831

A worn sign on Forbury Hill commemorates one man's efforts to improve the condition of the Forbury in the days before it was owned by Reading Corporation. The sign probably dates from the 1830s and was originally sited on the hill, although for a while it was relocated elsewhere.

The open space called the Forbury was originally the outer or public court of the Abbey, within the wall and gates but outside the monks' private area that was accessed through the Inner Gate. It covered a much greater area than the current Forbury Gardens, spreading further to the west and north. After the dissolution of Reading Abbey in 1539, the crown owned the land, which then eventually passed into private ownership.

In spite of not being common land, the Forbury remained an important area for the residents of the town, especially for holding the fairs that took place there each year.[87] John Man, writing in 1816, went further:

> Since the dissolution of the abbey, the Forbury has been considered by the inhabitants as common; for though this spot, with other of the abbey lands, is let by the crown to private individuals who consider it as freehold, yet the town has a prescriptive right, not only to hold fairs in it, but to use it as a place of amusement and exercise. This right both the corporation and the inhabitants have always been tenacious of preserving.[88]

The Town Charter granted by Queen Elizabeth in 1560 did indeed specify that the Forbury was to be used for fairs, by this time numbering four a year. The right for the public to use it as a place of amusement and exercise, however, was not mentioned.

The custom and practice of treating the land as if it were common was challenged in 1776, when Rev John Spicer, formerly Head Master of Reading School,[89] took matters into his own hands. No doubt during his tenure he had been bothered by this public use, as the school, which bordered the Forbury, used it as a playground for the boys. Following his retirement, however, his annoyance had grown; he had bought a house in the Forbury and probably felt that the public were in his front garden and, of all things, playing cricket!

FORBURY HILL.
THE BEAUTIFYING OF THIS HILL
AND OTHER IMPROVEMENTS IN
THE FORBURY WERE MADE A.D.
1831 UNDER THE DIRECTION
OF JOSHUA VINES ESQ[R]
WHO RAISED A SUBSCRIPTION FOR
THAT PURPOSE AND SUPERINTENDED
THE WORK.

He placed the following advertisement in the *Reading Mercury*:

READING, June 6, 1776.

Whereas the Pasture Land in the outer court of the Abbey, called the Forbury, is private property, and subject to public use only during the continuance of the fairs, as recited in the charters of queen Elizabeth and king Charles I to the Corporation of Reading, though many persons have erroneously asserted it to be common to the inhabitants in general, at all times of the year; and whereas the said Forbury has been improved at great expence with the view of ornament and doing credit to the town, and such intention is frustrated by persons playing there at Cricket, to the great annoyance of passengers and damage of the pasture, all persons offending are desired to forbear such practice for the future or their pretended claim will be disputed in due course of law, by me,

JOHN SPICER.[90]

Spicer's advertisement appeared again the following week, and immediately below it was a riposte from one or more of the townsfolk:

READING, June 15, 1775 [an error for 1776] CRICKET
On Monday next will be played in the FORBURY,
A GRAND MATCH at CRICKET,
By GENTLEMEN resident in this Borough.

On which Occasion, a superb Tent will be erected on FORBURY HILL; on the Summit of which will be displayed the Ensign of Liberty — Elegant Accommodation will be provided for such Ladies and Gentlemen as chuse to regale themselves on that agreeable Spot.

The preference of the Subscribers to the late Improvements, is particularly desired.

The Wickets to be pitched at Two

Beneath this advertisement was a special message for Rev John Spicer:

The most respectful Compliments are presented to the Rev. Mr. S—r, earnestly entreating the Honour of his Company to partake of a cold Collation on the Hill, where a proper Apparatus will be previously prepared for a commodious Survey of the adjacent Country, in order to afford him a desirable Opportunity of making Choice of whatever Extent his *Modesty* may esteem worthy appropriating, as an Addition to his *lately acquired private Property* in the Forbury.[91]

Unfortunately, the next issue of the *Reading Mercury* is missing from the Reading Library collection so it remains uncertain what happened next! It seems, however, that Mr Spicer must have quietly dropped his opposition to games of cricket on the Forbury, although no doubt retaining his irritation as he looked out from his 'lately acquired property.'

When Dr Valpy became Head Master of Reading School a few years later, there was contention between the boys of the school and of the town over the use of the Forbury – see Chapter XVI.

Forbury Hill was almost certainly a product of the Civil War defences in 1643, partly created using stone and rubble from the old Abbey. Stories of it being the site of a 12th-century castle persist, but modern research suggests this is very unlikely.[92] Before the Forbury was owned by Reading Corporation, the Hill and its surroundings were often neglected and in a poor state. John Spicer's advertisement in 1776 quoted above stated that there had been work carried out to improve the Forbury 'with the view of ornament and doing credit to the town.' Those works had been those carried out by a Mr Stevens. In 1774, the *Reading Mercury* carried the advertisement:

> At the Town Hall in Reading on Tuesday the 2nd of August next, will be a BALL, in order to raise money for Mr Stevens to carry on his IMPROVEMENTS in the FORBURY, for the pleasure of the Public. To begin exactly at Seven o'Clock.
>
> Tickets to be had of Mr Stevens, at the Printing-Office, and at the Town Hall, at Three Shillings each.[93]

In the late 1790s further improvements were carried out, particularly to Forbury Hill. However, as often seems to be the case, not everyone valued the amenity:

> That beautiful spot, Forbury-Hill, having been lately embellished with railing, &c. at a considerable expence, and which was cheerfully defrayed by the voluntary contributions of the inhabitants of this town, we were lamenting to see the depredations that have been made on it within these few evenings, by some persons who have been observed to be loitering about, most probably for this mischievous purpose; we have now, however, the satisfaction of knowing, that the Magistrates of the Borough are determined to make an example of anyone that may in future be detected in thus wantonly destroying this pleasing accommodation to the public.[94]

The Forbury and its hill benefited greatly in the early 1800s from the attentions of Francis Annesley, MP for Reading from 1790 to 1806. Following his death in April 1812, an anonymous poem of 392 lines, *Forbury Hill*, was published, 'inscribed to the memory of the late Francis Annesley, Esq.'[95] An early stanza, having celebrated the hill as 'our pride, our bulwark, our defence,' and a time when 'thy walks were gravell'd neat / When thy smooth turf allur'd soft feet,' ends with a lament now that Annesley is gone:

> How chang'd alas! for he lies low,
> Whose hand has often bound thy brow;
> Who fenc'd thee round with palisade,
> Who deck'd thy verdant colonnade,

> And bade the bench inviting rise,
> Round thy fair elms of stately size.

The poet then takes in the view from the top of the hill around the four points of the compass, except for 'one ugly feature we pass by, / 'Tis horror to the feeling eye.' This was the view of the old 1793 Reading Gaol, not the 1844 building by George Gilbert Scott that, though altered, remains.

Towards its end, the poem looks to the hill's uncertain future:

> And thou, poor Mount! how shall thou fare the while?
> Will no protecting safeguard bid thee smile?
> No friendly hand arise to fence thee round?
> To heal thy deep distresses none be found?
> Shall not some peer of him so low that lies,
> Some other Phoenix from his ashes rise?

In due course, one such 'Phoenix' would be Joshua Vines. However, before him, in February 1817 the Corporation took the unusual step of becoming involved in the hill's maintenance. By this date, the weather had been atrocious for a long time – now thought to be because of the eruption in 1815 of Mount Tambora in Indonesia. The result was agricultural disaster across the world in the year that followed. The Reading diarist, author of *Reading Seventy Years Ago*, chronicled some of the local difficulties in 1816:

April 15   This morning the ground was froze as hard as in the middle of winter

May 14   This month has hitherto been very cold and stormy; this morning the ice was about one-eighth of an inch thick

June 1   The weather has been this month like the preceding ones, unseasonably cold; there has scarce been a night without frost, vegetation is in consequence very backward

July 19   The weather still continues wet; the farmers are now taking up the clover hay and throwing it on the dunghill

September 5   That this summer has been the coldest ever remembered is an observation affirmed by everyone, but the last fortnight has been more particularly so; this morning the ice was nearly an inch thick; in the day we had snow, hail and rain

Many found it impossible to get work. Some left to seek their fortune in America, while others, skilled men included, took jobs shovelling gravel, or those who were less fortunate took to 'rambling about from morning to night in search of a job.'[96]

The Corporation employed 100 men in improving the Forbury. By mid-February 1817, in spite of rain and widespread flooding, they had repaired the roads and pathways around the Forbury and erected a wall around the hill. It was thought expedient to install a drain to take off waste water, in place of the ditch, which had become a nuisance to the town.

Unfortunately, the project ran out of capital and the Corporation issued handbills asking for help to raise the £120 needed to complete the project and keep the men employed for a further month. However, Mr J. Blagrave and Mr H. Vansittart, tenants of the land under the crown, stepped in and threatened the organising committee with an action for trespass and consequently the work had to stop.[97]

Over ten years later Forbury Hill was again in need of repair and on this occasion it fell to Joshua Vines, as he approached his 70th birthday, to be its preserver. Joshua was born in 1761 in Brinkworth, Wiltshire. He moved to Reading in the early 1790s to join his older brother David, who ran a successful shop in Broad Street described in its advertisements in the *Reading Mercury* as 'Cheese-Factors, Bacon- Sellers, and Coal-Merchants.'[98] In 1795, the same year as he married, Joshua became sole owner of the business, with the partnership between the brothers dissolved by mutual consent.[99]

Over the next 35 years both his business and his family prospered, the latter with the addition of three daughters and a son. Then on 10 March 1830 his wife Anne died, aged 59, 'sincerely beloved and lamented by her family and friends.'[100] It was following this bereavement that Joshua began his great work of restoring Forbury Hill. By November of the same year, the *Reading Mercury* commended:

> ... the public spirit of Mr. Joshua Vines, who with a liberality that does him the highest honour has actually contributed both bodily labour and private expence towards repairing an ornament, which it is a reproach to the town to have so long been suffered to crumble away under the mischievous pranks of idle boys. It is earnestly recommended to our fellow-townsmen to support the generous endeavour of Mr. Vines, by subscribing towards an iron railing, without which support his work will soon be trodden down by cattle, and mischievous children, and his labours rendered in vain.[101]

The people of Reading responded to the call and by mid-February of the following year had contributed £93 of the required £125 to pay for the railing. The work to erect it began shortly after.[102] By May, the *Reading Mercury*, in rather flowery language, paid a lengthy tribute both to the work done and to the view from the top:

> As admirers of every real improvement in or about Reading, we have great pleasure in noticing the greatly improved and improving state of Forbury Hill, under the superintendence of Mr. Joshua Vines. Independently of the many advantages that the inhabitants, and especially the invalids of Reading, will derive from the renovation of this charming spot, it will prove doubly attractive to those who occasionally visit the town, for it has frequently been lamented that no care was taken of the most pleasant

promenade near Reading. Mr. Vines, we understand, has met with every encouragement on the part of his fellow townsmen that warranted him to proceed; and we now trust, that as further subscriptions are required to reimburse Mr. V. a considerable sum that he is in advance, that the same liberal spirit will manifest itself for the completion of that which has been so well begun. Much might be said in commendation of the scene which from the hill's summit swells before the enraptured gaze of the spectator. It is a prospect of uncommon beauty during the summer and autumn and cannot be passed 'in tameless transport by,' even by those who reside near and have frequent views of it. The stranger who first visits the spot must acknowledge its grandeur, and if only he be duly acquainted with the history of the place, cannot fail of being highly gratified. The neat little village of Caversham is seen to particular advantage, with its white steepled church shaded by verdant woods; and its mansion encircled and backed by timber of superior size. And there also the Thames is seen to 'drag its slow length along,' from whose banks the ground gradually rises, clothed in all the luxuriance of nature. Westwardly are clumps of thickly-studded firs, whose sombre tints are finely relieved by the rich green of the pasture lands beneath, which, joining the wide open valley usually called the King's-mead, spread eastwardly till checked by the junction of the Thames and Kennet; beyond which, Sonning and Shiplake hills 'in beauteous order terminate the scene.' The ruins of Reading's once magnificent abbey, 'defac'd by time and tott'ring in decay,' add greatly to the variety of the scene, and contribute to render it all a place of no ordinary interest.[103]

This great work of renovation was completed in 1831, as shown by the sign pictured at the start of the chapter. Interestingly, the work fell between Joshua's first wife's death and his second marriage, to Harriet Stevens of Watlington House, widow of John Stevens, on 20 October 1831.[104] I cannot find whether the Mr Stevens who carried out renovation of the Forbury in the 1770s is any relation to this family.

A couple of years later a minor controversy arose with the accusation that Joshua Vines had planted two oak saplings on Forbury Hill, thus compromising the view in the future as these trees grew. The writer of a letter to the *Reading Mercury* (who identified himself as 'C') railed:

> How Mr. V. could be persuaded to think that these trees, particularly oak, would be a further improvement, is not for me to decipher; indeed, I think it would puzzle the most scientific draftsman to solve the question...

> ... the present landscape scenery opening to view between the two noble clumps of elms, and increasing in beauty to the eye of the spectator as he advances on the southern footpath, will, in the course of a few years, if these obstructions are allowed to remain, be completely shut out and

exchanged – and for what? A dead, unmeaning blank, bringing with it inevitable destruction to the open, airy, and health-giving pasture now so much enjoyed, and so deservedly appreciated.[105]

Happily for Joshua Vines' reputation, this allegation was untrue. Two weeks later, a small insert in the same newspaper stated: 'In reply to the letter of a correspondent inserted on the 8th inst., we are requested to state that Mr. Joshua Vines was no party in planting the oak saplings on Forbury-hill.' [106]

The only reference I can find to the sign on Forbury Hill is the following, dating from 1852. During a meeting of the Town Council, the Town Clerk stated:

> The late Mr. Joshua Vines put up a tablet in front of Forbury Hill, and Mr. Wheble made him take it away, and it was subsequently placed above the Abbey arch.[107]

Perhaps this tablet was the sign that we have now, put up not by Mr Joshua Vines, but in thanks to him for his much-appreciated work and restored to its proper location.[108]

VI. Henry West 1840

The memorials to Henry West in St Laurence's churchyard and on Reading Station state that he died in unusual circumstances on 24 March 1840.

The *Reading Mercury* proudly announced in its edition of 21 March 1840 that the long-awaited opening of the Great Western Railway to Reading would be on Monday 30 March.[109] The *Berkshire Chronicle* added a little more detail, that 'the second portion of the line of rails is in a great forwardness, and the offices of the station are fast assuming a form suitable for carrying on the immense business of the establishment.'[110]

This announcement followed the partial opening of the line the previous week when the Chairman, Mr Charles Russell, and the Directors of the Great Western Railway company had made the journey from London to Reading, behind the *Evening Star* locomotive. They inspected the progress of the works at the station and then sat down to a meal before returning.[111]

The station area was no doubt very busy as the workforce made every effort to complete the works needed before the opening. The weather had been cold in the days up to Sunday 22 March, and then it turned to rain, all day Sunday through to Monday. However, happily for the Great Western Railway workers, by Tuesday morning it was again fine, although becoming very windy.

Work was progressing on glazing the roof of a large building – the passengers' shed, variously reported as 150 feet or 200 feet long – just behind the Station House. Then at about 3.30pm there was a 'sudden and violent gust of wind' which tore off much of the roof of the shed and carried it away, despite its weight of approximately four tons.

Unfortunately, one workman – Henry West, a carpenter – was taken with the roof. Other workmen saw him clinging on desperately as the roof flew along and then smashed into another building. The roof shattered into pieces and Henry West was thrown further – in all the wind had carried him some 200 feet. Fellow workers ran to help him, but Henry did not regain consciousness and is thought to have died as he hit the ground or very shortly after. There were several others injured at the same time, but only one seriously. This was Mr Thomas Grissell, one of the partners in Grissell & Peto, civil engineering contractors, who received a severe wound to the head due to falling bricks.

Henry's body was carried the short distance to the Boar's Head in Friar Street (a 17th-century building now sadly demolished). Later that evening an inquest was held at the Public Office, before J.J. Blandy, coroner, and 'a respectable

Memorial to Henry West in St Laurence's churchyard

jury'. A verdict of accidental death was returned. There remains some confusion over the deceased's name: the coroner (and the local newspapers) called him William West, but both the parish record of his burial and the memorial raised by his friends called him Henry.[112] Henry's funeral took place on Sunday 29 March. The *Reading Mercury* reported:

The late Accident at the Railway Station. —

The remains of the unfortunate man (William West) whose untimely death was occasioned at the Reading Station of the Great Western Railway, by the hurricane of Tuesday se'nnight, were deposited in St Lawrence's Church-yard on Sunday afternoon last, and a more affecting scene than was exhibited on that occasion we have seldom witnessed in this town.

Between forty and fifty of his fellow workmen at the above works (principally carpenters) evinced their affectionate esteem for their departed companion, by following him in mourning attire to the grave, and by having, we understand, contributed a small sum each towards the payment of the funeral expenses. At about five o'clock, the procession, preceded by two mutes, started from the Boar's Head Inn, Friar-street (where his body was originally taken) and proceeded, two abreast, slowly to the church-yard, where the burial service was read, in the presence of a vast concourse of spectators, by the Rev. W.W. Phelps, curate of St Lawrence's Church. The rev. gentleman afterwards addressed the assembly in an impressive and highly appropriate exhortation, which was, apparently, most attentively listened to by them.[113]

Henry West was a 24-year old, unmarried journeyman carpenter from Wilton in Wiltshire. The memorial shown at the beginning of this chapter states:

IN MEMORY OF HENRY WEST
Who lost his life in a WHIRLWIND at the
GREAT WESTERN RAILWAY STATION READING
on the 24th of March 1840
Aged 24 years

Sudden the change, in a moment fell
And had not time to bid my friends farewell,
Yet hushed be all complaint, 'tis sweet, 'tis blest,
To change Earth's stormy scenes for Endless rest,
Dear friends prepare, take warning by my fall,
So shall you hear with joy your Saviour's call.

A Rail was erected at the time by his fellow workmen
as a token of affectionate respect to his memory.

The memorial board itself is the 'Rail' mentioned, as according to the *Oxford English Dictionary*, a rail can be 'a horizontal bar of wood or metal, fixed upon upright supports (posts) as part of a fence.' This was no doubt a common usage among Henry's carpenter friends.

The memorial goes on to state that it was renewed by Henry's brother George in 1862 and then by his niece F. G. Rixon in 1924. Reading Corporation then renewed it in 1971. There is a very similar oak board on display at the National Railway Museum at York, which had originally been at Reading Station.[114] The Railway Heritage Committee has designated this memorial as 'of sufficient interest to warrant preservation' so it has a protected status. In 1994, Reading Borough Council and Regent Inns plc erected a plaque on platform 7 of Reading Station.[115]

An interesting difference between the three memorials is that the one in St Laurence's churchyard has missed out the word 'I' in the second phrase: 'Sudden the change, I in a moment fell.' Both of the other memorials include it.

On the day following Henry's funeral, the opening of the Great Western Railway Station at Reading went without any further hitch. The first train, drawn by the locomotive *Fire Fly*, departed for London at 6 o'clock. There were not many passengers that early in the morning! The first arrival, greeted by huge crowds for some distance along the line and in the Forbury, was at 9.15, having taken an hour and a quarter (including stops) to do the journey from London. In all, eight trains arrived and nine departed from the station on its first day, and all operations went smoothly. The fastest train that first week was on the Thursday afternoon, which covered the distance from London to Reading in an hour and five minutes, having stopped five times along the way.[116]

With the coming of the train to Reading, the town would not be quite the same place ever again.

VII. Drinking Fountain 1860

The drinking fountain built against the south wall of St Laurence's Church tower was donated to the town by Thomas Rogers and was opened on 27 July 1860.[117]

The first public drinking fountain installed in England was erected in Liverpool in March 1854, on the initiative of Charles Pierre Melly. A count at this drinking fountain soon after its opening found that 2,886 persons drank there in a twelve-hour period. Encouraged by its success, Melly installed six more in the city by the end of the year.[118] Soon many other councils and philanthropists were emulating Liverpool by installing their own drinking fountains. The first one in London was opened on 21 April 1859 outside St Sepulchre's Church, Holborn.[119]

With a constant supply of clean water now readily available in our country, it is hard to comprehend what a difference a drinking fountain made. For the majority of people in 1860, if they were thirsty, they would need to go to a public house and drink beer or something similar. The availability of water safe to drink changed that, much to the delight of Temperance Societies.

Before Reading's first drinking fountain, there was a town pump in Market Place next to the Simeon Memorial, but by the late 1850s it had fallen into disrepair, with arguments over who bore the responsibility to pay for its restoration.[120] There is a possibility that a drinking fountain, erected at William Isaac Palmer's expense, was installed in the Forbury in 1859, but it is more likely that it was talked of in 1859 but not installed until August 1861.[121]

Thomas Rogers was Clerk to the Reading Local Board of Health. He commissioned a design for a drinking fountain to be installed at his own expense, and gained approval from the Town Council in November 1859.[122] After initial thoughts of placing it in St Mary's Butts, it was decided instead to place it under Blagrave's Piazza beside St Laurence's Church.

The Piazza, generally known as 'Church Walk' was a six-arched covered arcade, built in 1619 (see Chapter II). However, to the distress of many in the town, it was demolished in May 1865, five years after the drinking fountain was installed. The public announcement was made on Saturday 20 May, and by the following Monday it was half removed.[123] Among the reasons given for its removal were that the Piazza had become a place for 'a nightly rendezvous for the idle and dissolute'[124] and thus a nuisance for the neighbourhood.

The design that Thomas Rogers chose for his drinking fountain was by Messrs Poulton and Woodman, architects, and was constructed by Messrs

Drinking Fountain against the south wall of St Laurence's Church tower

Wheeler, stonemasons, and made of Mansfield stone. The drinking fountain was described by the *Reading Mercury* as follows:

> The principal basin, which is semi-octagonal in outline, projects from the face of the stone a considerable distance, and bears upon the outer edge the text from Proverbs 16, 'The fear of the Lord is a fountain of life,' and is supported by a marble column. On each side of the column there is an arched recess, with small basins for animals, supplied with water from the overflow of the large basin. In the recess above the upper basin there is an elaborate piece of carving in imitation of the water lily, and nothing could be more perfect than the workmanship. From the point of a central leaf there issues a small jet of water which descends to the middle of the basin and above there is a double arched canopy, supported on marble columns with carved capitals. Upon the edge of this canopy there is an inscription recording the date of erection and the name of the donor. There is a neat little arched recess on each side of the fountain, for the purpose of placing the drinking cups.[125]

The opening ceremony was performed on Friday 27 July 1860 by the Mayor, Henry A. Simonds. Unfortunately, Thomas Rogers was not able to be present, due to what the newspapers termed a 'domestic affliction.' The Town Clerk, John Jackson Blandy, read a letter from Mr Rogers formally presenting the fountain to the town. The vicar of St Laurence's, Rev John Ball, responded with a prayer, which was followed by a short speech by the Mayor.

The Mayor thanked Mr Rogers and then the Water Works Company who had offered to supply the fountain with water free of charge. The Mayor then 'stepped forward and after filling one of the cups drank to the advancement of the public spirit which contributed such works to the town'. Although Mr Rogers was absent, he was represented by Dr Wells, who stated that:

> It was Mr. Roger's intention not merely to contribute to the comforts of his fellow citizens, especially the poorer portion of them, but he wished to give ready access to a refreshing drink to the weary wayfarer and traveller, in order that they might quench their thirst while passing through this town, and also to all who dwelt around, the means of obtaining a drink of pure and refreshing water, and who previously were obliged to have recourse to the public house. They all knew that intemperance was the great sin of the nation, and hitherto, he was afraid, there had been some excuse for it, in consequence of not providing the means of quenching the thirst by pure water. Henceforward he trusted that such a necessity for going into a public house would cease.

There was some concern at the opening ceremony that the drinking fountain would be vulnerable to damage by members of the public. However, the Mayor took comfort from the fact that just on the opposite corner from the

Piazza was the Compter House, where Mr Peck, the Police Inspector, and his colleagues were based.

Their concern seemed to be justified, as less than two weeks later the newspapers reported: 'A CUP AND CHAIN STOLEN FROM THE DRINKING FOUNTAIN.' The *Reading Mercury* continued:

> It must create a feeling of indignation in the mind of every respectable inhabitant of this town, to learn that on Thursday night last, one of the cups which was fastened by a brass chain to the drinking fountain, at St Lawrence's Church, was torn away, chain and all, from its fastening. Such a piece of wanton mischief cannot be too severely reprobated, and we sincerely hope that the perpetrator of such a disgraceful act will be discovered and undergo the greatest punishment the law will allow, and we are sure, if the culprit be apprehended, the magistrates will show him no mercy as all must feel he would be deserving of none. It is believed, and with good reason, that it is no inhabitant of Reading who committed the offence, but some of the ruffians who attended the races.[126]

The fountain is now rather a shadow of its former self. It has lost its finial, which had made the whole 14 feet (about 4.3 metres) tall. The various inscriptions described above have all disappeared. There was a crest on the 'gable', which has now been replaced by a Berkshire stag (or possibly a reference to Psalm 42 verse 1: 'As the deer pants for streams of water, so my soul pants for you, my God'). It is a Grade II Listed building.[127] Following its restoration, a brass plaque was attached to the west side of the fountain:

Fountain Erected 1860
Restored in 1990 by
Reading Borough Council
and
Thames Water
Working Together in Partnership

VIII. The Maiwand Lion 1886

The Maiwand Lion was unveiled on 18 December 1886. It commemorates the gallantry of those of the 66th (Berkshire) Regiment who gave their lives at 'Girishk, Maiwand and Kandahar and during the Afghan Campaign' and in particular the battle of Maiwand on 27 July 1880.

The Second Anglo-Afghan War started in late 1878 and continued until the decisive British/Indian victory at Kandahar in September 1880. Her Majesty's 66th (Berkshire) Regiment of Foot was deployed to Afghanistan from India in early 1880.[128] It formed part of the 1st Brigade of the 1st Division, Kandahar Field Force, and was under the overall command of Brigadier-General George Scott Reynolds Burrows.

The Brigade was ordered from Kandahar to march to support Sher Ali Khan, known as the Wali, Governor of Kandahar, who was asking for a force to bolster his authority and stop his Afghan troops deserting to the enemy, Ayub Khan.[129] The 66th Regiment set out on 5 July, under its commander Lieutenant-Colonel James Galbraith, on an 80-mile march to the Helmand River, where the Wali's army was encamped.

With the enemy getting closer, it was decided to disarm the Wali's army, which unsurprisingly resulted in most of them mutinying to join Ayub Khan, taking artillery and weapons with them. General Burrows pursued the mutineers to recapture their guns, catching up with them at Girishk. The action that followed resulted in the mutineers fleeing, abandoning their baggage and their artillery.[130]

Some days later, Ayub Khan was reported to be advancing towards Kandahar through the Malmund Pass and on via Maiwand. General Burrows decided to try to reach Maiwand before Ayub Khan and to stop his advance on Kandahar there.

On 27 July, the Brigade, about 2,500 strong, marched to Maiwand, arriving at 10.30am, only to discover that Ayub Khan was already in possession of the field. The British believed the enemy army to number about 6,000, but it was actually nearly 20,000. The British artillery were also outgunned, with 12 guns to the enemy's 30.

The 66th (Berkshire) Regiment quickly formed a rectangle on the extreme right of the British battle lines, with the enemy forming a vast horseshoe around the Brigade. The Berkshire's battle strength was five Companies, totalling 15 officers and 364 men, with another Company of 3 officers and 63 men detailed to guard the baggage in the rear. The Regiment also had had one officer and 46 men re-deployed to man the artillery guns that had been captured at Girishk.

The Maiwand Lion, Forbury Gardens

The battle started immediately and raged until 5pm. By the end of the battle about 2,500 Afghan soldiers and 969 British and Indian soldiers had been killed. The Brigade were continually overwhelmed throughout the afternoon by the numbers of Afghan warriors. It seemed that no matter how many were shot down, more replaced them.

The British/Indian line had held until about 2pm, but it began to buckle, mainly due to a lack of ammunition, as the enemy had circled around behind the lines and cut off the forces from their supply. From the left end, the battle line started to crumble, regiment by regiment, as the enemy pressed more and more heavily from the front, side and rear. Finally, just the Berkshires were left holding the line.

About 3.30pm the order was given for the Berkshires to retreat, which they managed to accomplish in good order using the cover provided by a nearby village. Following attempts to make a stand against the enemy, and with little ammunition left, a full retreat was ordered and most of the survivors escaped to follow the rest of the retreating soldiers heading for Kandahar.

However, 11 men, who probably remained to provide covering fire to enable the rest to escape, fought on, initially from a walled garden. Then, leaving the garden, they moved out into the open to face the enemy. No observer from the British army saw what happened next, but an Afghan Colonel wrote an eyewitness account:

> These men charged out of the garden and died with their faces to the foe, fighting to the death. Such was the nature of their charge, and the grandeur of their bearing, that although the whole of the Ghazis were assembled around them, no one dared approach to cut them down. Thus, standing in the open, back to back, firing steadily and truly, every shot telling, surrounded by thousands, these officers and men died; and it was not until the last man was shot down that the Ghazis dared to advance upon them. The conduct of these men was the admiration of all that witnessed it.[131]

The siege of Kandahar by Ayub Khan's army began on 6 August and was relieved by Lord Roberts on 31 August. The next day, Lord Roberts took the fight to Ayub Khan, his army joined by, among others, the 66th Regiment. At the Battle of Kandahar, Ayub Khan's forces were comprehensively defeated and put to flight, bringing the Second Afghan War to an end.

In Reading, the news of the terrible defeat at Maiwand gradually emerged, starting with the newspapers on 31 July, which first reported an 'annihilation' of General Burrows's force, but later downgraded it to a 'severe loss' of men.[132] The loss of the Regimental Colours was reported in early August. The Colours had been captured by the Afghan army and were never recovered. A telegram from Kandahar on 7 August stated that 'the majority of the officers of the 66th Regiment were killed defending the Colours, which were lost, as were also those of the Grenadiers.' [133] Following Maiwand, the Army, deciding that carrying regimental Colours was actually a disadvantage to a regiment, decreed that no Colours were to be taken into battle again.

By the end of October 1880, with many of the dead having been named in the newspapers, the first suggestion came forward from F. J. Crapp, Late Quartermaster Sergeant, 1st Berkshire Rifle Volunteer Corps, for a memorial stained-glass window in St Mary's Church, with a brass plate recording the names of the fallen.[134] The window was installed on Saturday 22 July 1882:

> On Saturday last the memorial window to the memory of the officers and men of the 66th (Berkshire) Regiment who fell in the Afghan campaign, was placed in St Mary's Church in this town. It had been hoped that a special service would have been held to unveil the window, but this was rendered impossible owing to the 1st Battalion of the Berkshire Regiment (49th) being ordered to Egypt; and it was therefore put up without any special service...
>
> The window, which is one of the most perfect specimens of mural fine art work that we have ever seen, has been designed by Messrs. Clayton and Bell.[135]

The window depicts 'Joshua meeting the Lord of Hosts' from the Biblical book of Joshua Chapter V. Beneath the window is written: 'To the glory of God and to the honoured memory of 11 officers and 317 non-commissioned officers and men of the 66th (Berkshire) Regiment who fell during the campaign in Southern Afghanistan in 1879 and 1880.'

It was not until mid-November 1880 that the story of the heroic Last Stand of the Eleven men of the 66th became known in Reading. The *Reading Mercury* reported:

> THE DISASTER AT MAIWAND.
> THE 66TH (BERKSHIRE) REGIMENT.
>
> The Calcutta correspondent of the Times gives a summary of a further instalment of despatches which have appeared in the Gazette of India respecting the late fighting in Southern Afghanistan. The correspondent says:–
>
> 'The most interesting of these is a letter dated October 1, from General Primrose to the Adjutant-General, giving details of the gallant and determined stand made by the 66th at Maiwand... They nearly all fell fighting desperately for the honour of their Queen and country. The General adverts at some length to the stand made by 100 men in a garden, and states, on the authority of a Colonel of Artillery in Ayoob's army, that when only 11 out of the 100 were left they charged and died with faces to the foe, fighting to the death... The 11 stood in the open, back to back, firing steadily and truly... till the last man was shot down.'[136]

By early 1881 suggestions began to be made for a further commemoration of the 66th Regiment's fallen in addition to the planned stained-glass window in St Mary's Church. The first suggestion of a statue that I can find is a letter to the editor of the *Reading Mercury* in February from Captain George C. Fowler, R. N., of Brimpton:

> SIR,— I have waited for some more influential pen than mine to bring before your readers the suggestion that the County of Berks might take honourable notice of Her Majesty's 66th Regiment, now returning to England. Would it not be well in these times when it is considered desirable to attach localised regiments to their county, to erect by subscription, in the Market-place, Reading, a Memorial Group, in imperishable bronze, to the glorious memory of those who fought and fell in the Battle of Maiwand, of whose heroism we are all so proud? I should feel it a privilege to add my mite for such a purpose.[137]

By September, a committee had been formed and the following advertisement appeared in the local newspapers:

> SIXTY-SIXTH REGIMENT.— It is proposed to place a MEMORIAL in READING to the Officers, Non- Commissioned Officers and Men of the 66th Regiment who fell during the Afghan Campaign of 1880. Messrs. Cox and Co., Craig's-court, have kindly consented to receive any SUBSCRIPTIONS from Officers formerly in the Regiment, or other friends who may wish to join. Suggestions from subscribers will be laid before the Committee.
> J. T. READY, Lt.-Colonel, President of Committee.
> Parkhurst, Isle of Wight, 30th August, 1881.[138]

By January 1882 the subscription list had been closed and the committee sought the advice of sculptor George Simonds, who suggested both the form of the memorial and its location – Forbury Gardens.[139]

George Simonds was a well-known sculptor, with a studio in Buckingham Palace Road, London. He was a local man, having been born in Bridge Street in Reading, and was the second son of George Simonds – the 'G' in H. & G. Simonds Brewery. He had taken up sculpture from an early age, studying and living in Germany, Belgium and Italy. By 1882, at almost 40 years old, he had an international reputation, especially for casting in bronze.

George Simonds began a series of studies of the lions at London Zoo. In June 1884 he exhibited a life- sized lion statue, a model for the memorial, at the Royal Academy.[140] The local myth that has grown that the sculptor got the gait of the lion wrong is incorrect, and neither did George Simonds end his life because of the supposed error – he lived on until 1929. Another local myth claims that the lion has no tongue, but this is not true either.

Meanwhile he was busy on the lengthy process of designing and casting the pieces in iron, at three times life size, for the colossal figure itself, as well as overseeing the production of the large pedestal.

Messrs Wheeler of Reading, in a specially erected workshop at their premises in Coley, produced the pedestal, using rich red clay to produce the terracotta blocks.[141] In August 1885 the work began to erect the pedestal in Forbury Gardens. The base measured 23ft 2½in long by 8ft 7in wide and 12ft 6in high. The erection of the base was completed on 23 January 1886.[142]

The eight separate pieces of the lion, cast by Messrs H. Young & Co. of Pimlico, were brought together and joined on the pedestal by December 1886.[143] The completed statue was truly huge: over 32ft from tip of the nose to tip of the tail and 13ft 4in from the forepaw to the top of the mane.

The unveiling ceremony, presided over by the Lord Lieutenant of Berkshire (Lord Wantage V.C.), took place at 2.30pm on Saturday 18 December 1886. A stand accommodated about 150 ladies and an enclosure was provided for invited guests. The survivors of the Battle and current members of the 66th Regiment were also present. An immense gathering of the public filled the rest of the Forbury.

The Lord Lieutenant, following a speech that rehearsed the events of the Battle, removed the Union Flag that was draped over the memorial while the Guard of Honour (the Berkshire Volunteers) presented arms. The memorial was thus officially handed over to the Mayor (Arthur Hill) and Corporation.[144]

The pedestal had two large panels, one at each end, stating the details of the battles and the date of erection of the statue, with five smaller panels on each side containing the names of the 329 men of the 66th Regiment who died in the Afghan Campaign. Unfortunately, the terracotta panels began to weather quite badly, resulting in the names of the fallen becoming obliterated. In 1909 the Lord Lieutenant of Berkshire (J. Herbert Benyon) launched an appeal to restore it. Under a scheme proposed by Mr G. W. Webb, FRIBA., of Reading, the terracotta facing was encased in Portland stone, with metal panels reproducing the engravings on the original.[145]

The main plaque states:

> This Monument records the names and commemorates
> the valour and devotion of XI officers and
> CCCXVIII Non.Com. officers and men of the LXVI Berkshire
> Regiment who gave their lives for their country at
>
> GIRISHK, MAIWAND and KANDAHAR
> and during the Afghan campaign
> MDCCCLXXIX—MDCCCLXXX

> 'History does not afford any grander or finer instance of gallantry
> and devotion to Queen and Country than that displayed
> by the LXVI Regiment at the Battle of Maiwand
> on the XXVII July MDCCCLXXX.'
> Despatch of General Primrose.

At the other end of the base, the plaque states:

> Erected
> MDCCCLXXXIV by
> Residents in Berkshire
> and by the Comrades and Friends
> of those whose names
> are here recorded.

Note that, although the date given above is 1884, it was actually in 1886 that the memorial was erected and so should have had VI at the end not IV.

There are four sets of three panels on the long faces of the pedestal, recording the names alphabetically of all 329 who died. There is one panel with the names of the eleven officers, one with the thirty-five non- commissioned officers, and ten panels with the names of the 283 Privates.

Just visible beneath the hind leg of the lion are the names of the sculptor and the founders:

> GEO. SIMONDS SCULPTOR
> H. YOUNG & CO. FOUNDERS.

Following this commission, George Simonds also produced the statues of Queen Victoria and George Palmer for Reading. In 1905 George's elder brother Blackall Simonds died and, upon inheriting his estate, George acceded to his brother's request and added Blackall to his name, becoming George Blackall Simonds. Subsequently, in 1910, he took on the chairmanship of the family brewery business. He came out top in the Reading Libraries' 'Great People of Reading' poll in 2005.[146]

In Friar Street in Reading there is an old pub – *The Bugle* – with its sign being a bugler of the 66th Regiment. After Maiwand, the pub owners, Simonds Brewery, had the buckle of the bugler's belt altered to show 66 in order to make the connection clearer.

As a postscript to this chapter, when the first Sherlock Holmes story, *A Study in Scarlet*, was published – in Beeton's Christmas Annual in 1887 – Dr Watson is introduced on the first page as a veteran of the Battle of Maiwand. Although initially attached to the Fifth Northumberland Fusiliers as Assistant Surgeon at Kandahar, he was then attached to the Berkshires, 'with whom I served at the fatal battle of Maiwand.' Watson was struck by an enemy bullet in the shoulder and was rescued from 'the murderous Ghazis' by his orderly, who threw him across a packhorse and so brought him back to safety.

IX. Jubilee Memorial Fountain 1887

The Memorial Fountain in St Mary's Butts was opened on 18 June 1887 to commemorate Queen Victoria's Golden Jubilee.

Following the redevelopment of the St Mary's Butts area (see Chapter XI), the Town Council agreed at the end of January 1887 to seek designs for a drinking fountain to be erected in the central area of the road.[147] The following advertisement appeared on 4 February 1887:

> To ARCHITECTS AND OTHERS.
> The Corporation invite Architects and others who are willing to enter into a Competition, to Furnish Designs for the ERECTION of a PUBLIC FOUNTAIN in ST MARY'S BUTTS – the entire cost of which must not exceed £400. Should any of the Designs be selected, the Architect whose Design is adopted will be employed to carry out the work. Any further information may be obtained on applying to the undersigned, to whom all designs must be delivered not later than noon on Monday, the 21st inst.
> ALBERT W. PARRY
> The Borough Surveyor [148]

The detailed instructions to the competitors required the fountain not to exceed 15 feet by 22 feet and that the water was to drip from one level to another, and to provide a drinking fountain and a drinking place for dogs.

Meanwhile, the Reading Jubilee Committee, charged with deciding how the town would celebrate Queen Victoria's Golden Jubilee in June that year, agreed to fund half of the cost of the fountain from the public subscriptions they received. The other half was to come from the Council's coffers.[149]

With only 17 days between the advertisement for entries to the competition and the deadline for the designs, it is surprising that there were about 40 entries, from about 20 different entrants. To avoid bias, entries either went under a *nom de plume* or had the designer's name covered up. The committee unanimously chose a pair of designs under the motto 'Faith, Hope and Charity', which turned out to be by local Reading architect George W. Webb of 14 Friar Street. The committee were unsure which of the two designs to choose, but finally decided on the one shown overleaf.[150]

Mr Webb's other design was based upon a 'Mercat Cross' with an octagonal centre-piece supporting a single column, at the top of which was a figure of the 'Queen supporting the Universe, the whole being about 25 feet in height.' I wonder how the universe was represented.

The contract to build the fountain was placed with Messrs Wheeler Bros., of Reading, for the total price of £400. By May the 'Jubilee Fountain' was virtually finished and was being lead-lined by Messrs Sisley and Goodall.[151] The local newspapers went into considerable detail:

The foundation of the fountain is of concrete, which is taken down some distance below the road, to allow space for a subway, which is constructed from one side to the other, so that access can be had to any portion of the interior when required. A separate pipe and tap is used for each water supply, and the water can be drawn out of each pipe and basin and the whole left dry before the commencement of winter to prevent the action of frost. The lower basin is oval and occupies the whole of the space allowed. The north and south ends are paved with Wycombe paving, and at each of the four corners are red granite guard piers. It is the intention of the Corporation to place eight additional granite guard posts, with iron railing and gutter, to protect the fountain from being damaged by cattle, &c.; but owing to the great difficulty obtaining the granite in time the posts are not yet fixed. The moulded plinth coping, &c., are of solid Portland stone, and at the north and south ends drinking basins are sunk in the coping, and provided with cups and chains. The overflow from the basin is used to supply a stone trough for dogs below.

From the centre of the lower basin is raised a block of masonry, the external portion of which is composed of alternate bands of red Mansfield and white Portland stone, the central band having carved ornamentation representing the English rose, and the upper band water lilies in various stages from the bud to the flower. At equal intervals round the central block are eight polished Peterhead red granite columns, with carved capitals, each one being of a different design, the whole supporting a beautifully carved and moulded frieze, which forms the second basin; running round the frieze in bold relief letters is the following inscription: 'Erected to commemorate the fiftieth year of Her Majesty's reign, 1887.'

(In fact, the inscription is: Erected on the completion of the 50th year of the reign of Queen Victoria 1887.)

Above the inscription is a carved band representing the Shamrock and Thistle. At equal intervals between each column are eight carved gargoyles or grotesque heads, each one of a different design, and from the mouth of each a flat sheet of water is discharged into the basin below. From the centre of the second basin is raised a small oval block composed of bands of red Mansfield and Portland stone, surrounded by four small columns of polished granite, with carved capitals, supporting solid oval brown Portland stone, which is surrounded by 20 small water jets, each one playing up the stone and falling back over the edge below. This stone is encircled by a band of carving representing the British oak. On the top of the stone is placed a single polished red granite column, which

Jubilee Memorial Fountain with St Mary's Church behind

is surmounted by a carved capital, on which are two lions back to back, each with a shield, one bearing the Royal Arms and the other the Borough Arms; the side spaces being filled up with carved water lilies, bulrushes, &c. From the centre of the lions rises a white stone carved finial surmounted by a beautifully carved crown and coronet, from the centre of which is the top water jet.[152]

The opening of the fountain was the first event in over a week of celebrations to mark Queen Victoria's Golden Jubilee, from Saturday 18 to Sunday 26 June. Barriers were placed around the fountain to cordon off an enclosed seated area for invited guests, and a platform was erected. The Mayor, Arthur Hill, and Corporation robed in a nearby house and processed, behind the mace, to the fountain at 5pm. As they arrived, the town band played the National Anthem.

The Mayor then paid tribute to the work that had been done to clear St Mary's Butts, and to the generosity of Isaac Harrinson (see Chapter XI). Concluding his speech, the Mayor:

> ventured to express the hope that the fountain might for centuries remain in its present appropriate position, near the fine parish church of St Mary: an emblem of the water of life of which no man should thirst again who partook of it; a memorial of the Jubilee of Her Majesty's reign; a pleasing object to the eye; and satiating with its cooling stream the thirst of many a passer-by. It only remained for him to ask the Mayoress to turn on the water and declare the fountain open (cheers).

> The Mayoress then turned on the water by means of a wheel placed at hand, but only partially, because of the spray through the breeze which was blowing, and declared the fountain opened.

The guest of honour, Mr C.T. Murdoch MP, then addressed the gathering, echoing the Mayor's congratulations to all those who had brought such a great project to an impressive conclusion. After the ceremony:

> The fountain was then examined by the assemblage and the crowd, who had broken through the barriers, and after a time the gathering dispersed. Later in the evening the spot was visited by thousands of people. Mr. John Warrick's and most of the houses in the Butts near the fountain had been decorated in a manner suitable to the occasion and rendered the Butts quite attractive.

> Since the fountain has been opened it has been found that, either from a too great pressure of water or some other cause, the water is thrown much too far. The by-stander discovers that he is being sprinkled, and round the fountain there is a puddle. Steps should immediately be taken to remedy this state of things.[153]

It seems that the problem persisted for some time as several weeks later a question was raised at the Town Council meeting. The complainant stated that 'Nobody could go near it without getting their feet wet; the whole condition of it was most deplorable.'[154]

At some stage in its life, it ceased to be a fountain. Certainly, it needed to be turned off at least temporarily, awaiting repair, in 1903 as the condition of the lead lining had deteriorated badly.[155] For many years it has had a floral display in the lower of the basins.

The fountain has Grade II Listed status. The listing entry ends the description of the fountain with 'Water formerly spouted from the top and from the gargoyles' mouths. A typical Victorian amalgam of forms and conceits.'[156]

X. Queen Victoria's Statue 1887

The statue, standing near the Town Hall at the meeting of Blagrave Street and Friar Street, was unveiled on Wednesday 27 July 1887 to commemorate Queen Victoria's Golden Jubilee.

At a town meeting, convened at 3pm on Friday 3 December 1886 at the Old Town Hall in Reading, the Mayor, Arthur Hill, told the large gathering that the Council had agreed to focus on three things to celebrate Queen Victoria's Golden Jubilee: a permanent local memorial, namely a statue; a monetary contribution to the proposed Imperial and Colonial Institute; and a grand scheme for great popular rejoicing. The Mayor explained that since a statue could take up to a year to create and the Jubilee was only seven months away, the Council had already commissioned the statue. They had chosen the well-known Reading-born sculptor, George Simonds, whose huge Maiwand Lion was set to be unveiled a fortnight after this meeting.[157]

With little time in hand, therefore, George Simonds drafted his design for the Council. Following their approval, he built a model of the statue, which gained Her Majesty's approval by the beginning of April 1887.[158] Meanwhile Simonds had sent off one of his experienced workmen to the Cava Gioia quarry in Italy for a suitable sized block of Carrara marble, which had arrived at his London workshop in early January.[159]

The Borough Surveyor, Mr A.W. Parry, ensured that adequate foundations were provided at the agreed site near the new Town Hall.[160] A wooden version of the pedestal was placed in position and the Council were asked to decide which way the statue should face 'as the streets were not at right angles'.[161] They decided that the statue should look northwards along Blagrave Street, which at the time would probably have meant that the Queen was visible from passing trains. Personally, I think that, given that Her Majesty's head is turned very slightly to the right, she is actually keeping a close eye on the comings and goings from the main Town Hall entrance!

After much anticipation and a great deal of preparation, the Jubilee celebrations got underway on Saturday 18 June 1887 with the opening of the new fountain in St Mary's Butts. Good weather, which became known as 'Queen's weather', continued all week, adding to the sense of occasion, with Tuesday being Jubilee Day and a general holiday. All the planned events went off extremely well, except for one: the unveiling of the statue had to be postponed as arrangements were not yet quite ready.[162]

A month later, however, all was in place and the statue was erected on 26 July, ready for its unveiling the following day.[163] Although the Queen was not

Statue of Queen Victoria

to be present in person (and in fact never visited Reading in her life), she was to be represented by her first cousin, His Royal Highness Prince George, 2nd Duke of Cambridge. Upon his arrival by Great Western train at 11am, the Duke was escorted by a 60-strong guard of honour formed by the Royal Yeomanry Cavalry and Royal Berks Volunteers to a tour of Huntley & Palmers' Biscuit Factory, followed by the Market Place premises of Messrs Sutton & Sons.

Since the day happened also to be the seventh anniversary of the Battle of Maiwand, the Duke's entourage went next through the Forbury to view the Maiwand Lion, the memorial to those Berkshire men who fell in the Afghan campaign. From there the carriages took them to the Town Hall. In the Council Chamber, the Mayor read the official statement of welcome by the Council and presented the Duke with a ceremonial copy of the text in a decorative border (an 'illuminated address'), which was a 'striking and most beautiful work of art... illuminated by Mr W. H. Pountney.' The Duke of Cambridge gave a short speech of thanks in reply.

It was then time for the unveiling ceremony, and the procession made its way the short distance from the Town Hall to the statue. Behind the statue, on the south side of Friar Street (the side that now houses Marks & Spencer) a grandstand had been erected by Mr T. H. Blake, builder and decorator of King's Road. It was huge, 104 feet long (almost 32 metres) with six tiers, altogether seating 450 people – all specially invited by the Mayor. In addition, there were many thousands gathered around, who raised hearty cheers as the guard of honour gave a Royal Salute.

Managing such an event must have been something of a nightmare. Special road closures had been publicised, giving very restricted access to the roads around Blagrave Street, Friar Street and Market Place.[164] It later transpired that due to a communication problem (the new Superintendent of Police had only been in post two days after all) the police were not fully briefed and Mr Richard Benyon, Reading's High Steward, could not get to the unveiling ceremony as he was sent 'round and round'.[165] Happily he did manage to get to the lunch afterwards.

The ceremony began with the Rev J. M. Guilding, vicar of nearby St Laurence's, offering a special prayer, followed by the Lord's Prayer. Then the Mayor addressed the gathering:

Your Royal Highness, my Lords, Ladies and Gentlemen,

We are assembled today to witness and take part in the unveiling of a statue of our beloved Queen, which has been erected by the committee engaged in carrying out the Jubilee proceedings in Reading, and I, personally, am present as it were in a double capacity, first to hand over the statue on behalf of the committee, and secondly, as Mayor, to accept it on behalf of the town. It is with much satisfaction I have asked you to come together for the purpose today, because the occasion will be remembered by us with unusual pleasure, not only owing to the kindness of a member of the Royal family, so near to the person and the throne of Her Majesty, as H. R. H. the Duke of Cambridge in coming down to perform the ceremony for us, and thus surround the event with additional interest, but because, by Her Majesty's special permission, the Duke of Cambridge comes to us as directly representing her Majesty herself, who amid the overwhelming affairs of State, and other engagements which would tax the energies of a strong man, yet finds time to remember with sympathy and consideration our proceedings in the town Reading — a recognition for which I am sure you will all feel with me our gratitude is due.

The statue which is to be unveiled today has an additional value to Reading people as being the work of a Reading man — Mr George Simonds — who has already achieved considerable success as a sculptor both at home and abroad. I may remind you that we already possess in Reading one great work of his—the colossal lion erected in the Forbury in memory of the heroes who fell at Maiwand, a work which has been this day seen by H. R. H. the Duke of Cambridge, and in which I am sure he has felt a true soldier's interest — the more so, as, by a singular coincidence, this day is the anniversary of the battle of Maiwand, in memory of which it was erected. I hope and believe the statue now before us will be found to merit, and will deservedly receive, a favourable verdict at your hands, and long remain a conspicuous ornament to our town. It is handed over to us as the last of the permanent local memorials by which Reading marks the celebration of Her Majesty's Jubilee. You know we have had in Reading our local festivities and rejoicings for every class — for the young and for the old, for the rich and for the poor, enthusiastically carried out on a large scale — the remembrance of which is fresh on your minds, and will not be forgotten by the present generation, but when with us the recent festive celebration of Jubilee events shall have faded in the past, this record will remain to remind generations yet unborn of our appreciation of, and gratitude for, half a century of wise and beneficent reign, preserving, as it will do, for the benefit of those who follow us, a record of the features, so long familiar to us, of our well-loved Queen—a memento to be preserved with jealous care by our successors, of the great and wise and virtuous Sovereign who for so long a period has occupied the English throne. I will now ask his Royal Highness to kindly proceed to perform his function.

The Duke of Cambridge then unveiled the statue and the assembled thousands raised more hearty cheers. His Royal Highness replied to the Mayor's speech:

Mr Mayor, my Lords and Gentlemen, and Ladies, I feel extremely flattered and gratified by the wish expressed by the town of Reading that I should be here today to unveil Her Majesty's statue, and still more so that Her Majesty has authorised me to come in her name to perform this pleasing ceremonial. All I can say is that this great Jubilee of our Queen has produced an amount of loyalty, and good feeling, not only in this town of Reading but throughout the whole country and indeed the whole Empire, which must be gratifying to Her Majesty and to everybody who has a right spirit with regard to this great Empire. Among the many duties I have had to perform in connection with the Queen's Jubilee none has afforded me more gratification than to come to Reading to unveil so fine a statue as we see before us of Her Majesty the Queen.

Following the unveiling ceremony, the Mayor entertained the Duke of Cambridge and about 170 invited guests at an 'elegant luncheon (served to perfection by Mrs George, of the Queen's Hotel)' in the Town Hall.[166]

The statue and pedestal together are a little over 18 feet (about 5.5 metres) tall. Queen Victoria is represented crowned and in State robes, holding the sceptre in her right hand and the orb in her left. The front of the dress is covered with delicately executed brocade of an elaborate inter-twining pattern of rose, shamrock, and thistle. Her robe extends over the top of the pedestal on both sides and at the back. On the rear of the pedestal is written:

>ERECTED
>TO COMMEMORATE
>THE COMPLETION OF
>THE FIFTIETH YEAR OF
>HER MAJESTY'S REIGN
>JUNE 20TH 1887
>
>ARTHUR HILL, MAYOR

On the front of the pedestal is written:

>VICTORIA
>D: G:
>BRITANNIAR: REG:
>INDIAE IMP:
>FID: DEF:
>MDCCC
>LXXX
>VII

That is:

>Victoria
>by the Grace of God
>Queen of the British Territories
>Empress of India
>Defender of the Faith
>1887

Photographs of the event were taken by the Reading photographer Mr S. Victor White, of the Talbot Lodge Studios, Castle Street, and the Royal Victoria Studios, Blagrave Street. Queen Victoria's Private Secretary, Sir Henry Ponsonby, ordered copies of the photographs on Her Majesty's behalf a few days after the unveiling.[167]

The statue cost £1,000, which was entirely paid for by public subscription to the Reading Jubilee Fund.[168] However, the Council needed to fund a further £250 for lighting for the area as a street lamp had had to be removed in order to erect the statue.[169]

The story has grown over the years that the statue is positioned in such a way that the Queen has her back towards the town centre, and so in some way represents Her Majesty's rejection of the town. Since the decision about which way the statue would face was one taken by the Council, this is hardly likely. Rather, the direction the statue faces would mean that the Queen would be facing any official visitor to Reading, as they would arrive at the Town Hall.[170]

In January 2014, the statue was thoroughly cleaned as part of The Abbey Quarter Project. It has Grade II Listed status and interestingly, the listing entry incorrectly gives the statue's date as 1857. Its description, however, is a good one: 'Large Carrara marble statue of the Queen Empress in commanding and appropriate attire. High plinth with moulded cornice and base on wide step which has red granite corner bollards.'[171]

XI. Harrinson Testimonial Cross 1887

The cross in St Mary's churchyard was unveiled on 19 December 1887 as a testimonial to the generosity of Isaac Harrinson FRCS in helping to improve the parish of St Mary's and especially the clearance of St Mary's Butts.

Isaac Harrinson was born in Bardsey in Yorkshire in October 1810. Having become a Fellow of the Royal College of Surgeons, he moved to Reading in 1835 to be an assistant, later partner, to Mr George May.[172] Over the next 50 years Harrinson built up an extremely successful practice, becoming a wealthy man.[173] In April 1844 Harrinson married Ellen May, a relative of his partner,[174] and they lived for many years in Castle Street. In the early 1880s they moved to 'Bardsey', Bath Road. Ellen Harrinson died and was buried at St Michael's in Tilehurst in May 1885, aged 76.[175] Isaac Harrinson died on 26 June 1888, and was buried with his wife.[176]

Throughout his time in Reading, Harrinson attended St Mary's Church and, on several occasions, he used his fortune to benefit the parish. In 1865 he presented the stained-glass east window, still in place, to the church as a gift to the vicar.[177] In 1864 and in 1876 he contributed to improvements to the organ.[178] In 1872 he funded the building of the church's north aisle with a donation of £1,000, and also supplied it with copies of the Prayer Book and 'Hymns Ancient and Modern', all for the use of the poor of the parish.[179] A brass plaque in the north-west of the church commemorates this donation:

> To the Glory of God, and for the benefit of the poor
> of this parish, This Aisle was built by Isaac Harrinson of
> this parish, Surgeon, on condition that the seats therein
> 'be retained for their free use for ever'.
> This Aisle was consecrated by the Rt. Revd. John Fielder
> Lord Bishop of Oxford, October 17th 1872.
> Arthur P. Purey Cust. Vicar
> John Wells Hounslow
> John Bligh Monck. Churchwardens

In the middle of the 19th century, St Mary's Butts was a cluttered space. The church was screened from the road by a row of old houses and there was a set of dilapidated buildings in the middle of the lower part of the road, known as Middle Row, splitting St Mary's Butts into two narrow roads from Hosier Street to Castle Street.

Cross in St Mary's churchyard – Testimonial to Isaac Harrinson

The Town Council, in 1865, started to consider purchasing the houses in front of the church with a view to demolishing them and opening up the frontage to the church.[180] These houses were the John A'Larder almshouses (see Chapter I), originally built in the 15th century and rebuilt in 1775. The Charity Commissioners had agreed to allow the Consolidated General Almshouse Charities to sell the Almshouses in order to raise money for new almshouses in Castle Street.

The houses were described in a Town Council meeting by Mr Monck as having:

> ... no outlet or water-closet, and everything of an offensive character had either to be thrown through a hole the tenants might knock through the back of the house, or put down the main drain, and the buildings were, in his opinion, one of the greatest nuisances existing in the town.[181]

By December 1865 the purchase price for the 'five Almshouses on the south side of the entrance to St Mary's churchyard belonging to A'Larder's charity... and the other two Almshouses belonging to the same charity' had been agreed at £300.[182]

The Town Council, although now owning these seven tenements, did not take any action to improve the area by removing them. This was because they had a grander scheme in mind, involving the removal of the Middle Row houses as well. The cost of this part of the project was, however, beyond the Council's resources.

By early 1869, opinion in the town was firmly on the side of action. The contributor of 'Local Notes' in the *Berkshire Chronicle* thought that if St Mary's Butts were opened up and improved, some civic building erected in the centre of the space would be appropriate – public baths being his preference. He wrote:

> I refer to St Mary's Butts. This place, both on account of its central position and the junction of several streets, would be an excellent place of rendezvous; but at present a more unsightly street there is not in the town. After leaving the top of Broad Street you emerge into a wide thoroughfare, much too broad for practical purposes, and then suddenly the road diverges into two narrow ones, both of which are bounded on the sides by dilapidated buildings... It is perfectly clear that as long as those old houses stand in the middle of St Mary's Butts, the property around them will never be improved; and it is equally clear that if the houses are removed without something being put in their place there will be a very great waste of space. This site would not be broad enough if the houses were pulled down to allow the erection of a building such as I have alluded to, and leave a good street on each side of it; but then the site might be widened by removing that row of dilapidated houses adjoining St Mary's churchyard. The removal of these houses is desirable for several reasons.

They are not fit to live in, because there is not a back door to them; and for this reason as long as they stand as they do stand they will stand in their dilapidated state, for no one would go to the expense of rebuilding them as long as there is not a foot of space behind. Their removal would greatly improve the appearance of the neighbourhood by throwing open to view St Mary's Church and churchyard.[183]

Through the 1870s the matter was generally pushed down the order of priority by the very many projects that the Town Council were pursuing. In 1883, Isaac Harrinson offered £500 towards the purchase of the properties that would need to be bought. However, the chairman of the Town Council's Survey Committee, James Simonds, reported that the total purchase price of the properties would be in the region of an unaffordable £4250.[184]

In early 1884 the Council decided to launch an appeal for £1,000 (of which Harrinson's £500 would be half) to assist them to buy the necessary properties.[185] In order to expedite matters, by June 1885 Isaac Harrinson had improved his offer to the Council, but with a caveat: if the work was started without further delay, he would pay £500 when the work was begun, and a further £500 upon its completion. The Survey Committee 'felt that such a handsome offer should not be lost to the town.'[186]

In addition to the seven houses the Council already owned, a number of others needed to be purchased. By October 1886 the purchases were completed, with payments of:

£600 to the Trustees of the Church Charities for three houses at the northern end of Middle Row;
£300 to the Trustees of the General Charities for a house in the centre of the block;
£325 for four cottages in the block belonging to the Blagrave Estate; and
£1,515 for the transfer from the Church Land Charity for a house and premises fronting Castle Street.[187]

By the middle of November, the whole of Middle Row had gone, pulled down and cleared by the contractor, Mr B. Dunn of Crown Street, with the houses along the east, bordering St Mary's churchyard, following soon after.[188] Isaac Harrinson's payment of £1,000 if the work went ahead immediately had had the required effect!

The vicar and churchwardens of St Mary's Church announced in the following April that they would hold a 'Special Vestry meeting' to 'consider the best means of Publicly Recognising the Services rendered by Mr Isaac Harrinson in connection with the St Mary's Butts Improvements, and to adopt such course in relation thereto as may then be deemed expedient.'[189]

A very well-attended meeting decided upon presenting Mr Harrinson with an 'illustrated address', a written statement of their thanks within a decorative border, produced on vellum. In addition, the meeting proposed that a cross, bearing a record of Mr Harrinson's munificence, be erected in the churchyard on land where the houses had stood.[190] Designs were invited from Reading architects, and of the 14 received two were chosen by the organising committee and forwarded to Mr Harrinson, who chose which he preferred. This winning entry was a design by Mr Spencer Slingsby Stallwood.[191]

At noon on Monday 19 December 1887 the unveiling of the cross took place. Canon Garry, vicar of St Mary's, read the address given below, and with 'a few appropriate words' handed a ceremonial copy of the text to Mr Harrinson:

> 'That the inhabitants of St Mary's Parish, in public Vestry assembled, desire to record their high appreciation of the valuable aid rendered by Mr Harrinson in so liberally assisting in carrying out the improvements in St Mary's Butts, whereby dilapidated buildings have been removed and a great and lasting improvement secured.
>
> The Church Cross embodies this resolution in a permanent form, and will tell future generations of the munificence by which you have done so much to improve the fabric of St Mary's Parish Church, and to carry to a successful completion the improvements by which it can now be seen in its majestic dignity and proportions.
>
> We are, dear Mr. Harrinson,
> Yours faithfully,
> N. T. Garry, vicar,
> J. E. Sydenham & W. F. Blandy, Churchwardens.'

The design of the cross was based upon churchyard crosses from pre-reformation times, and is therefore in the style of English medieval architecture of the 15th century. It is octagonal, 14 feet in diameter at the base, and rising to a height of 20 feet. Above the three steps there are four panels bearing the shields of Mr Harrinson, the Borough of Reading, the Diocese of Salisbury (in which Reading was formerly) and the Diocese of Oxford (in which it is now). Near the top of the cross there is a band with the inscription 'By thy Cross and Passion, Good Lord, deliver us.'

Unfortunately, the main inscription is no longer legible. It used to say:

> *Erected*
> *by public subscription to record the munificence of*
> *ISAAC HARRINSON, ESQ.,*
> *by which the improvements in St. Mary's Butts*
> *were brought to a successful completion.*
> *A.D. 1887.*
> *The year of the Jubilee of Queen Victoria.*

On another step it used to say:

Architect – Mr. S. Slingsby Stallwood
Builders – Messrs. Wheeler

Isaac Harrinson lived only a further six months after this public demonstration of thanks. His obituary in the local newspaper recounted his many contributions to Reading life and society – he was for example a founder member of both the Reading Pathological Society and the Reading Philharmonic Society. The obituary ended with the following eulogy:

> Anything which tended to lighten or brighten the lives of people had his sympathy and ready help, and in furtherance of the Church of England Mr. Harrinson's zeal was unbounded. In politics Mr. Harrinson was an ardent Conservative. In many societies, in many different ways, his loss will be felt. No one could have been more liberal; no one could have been less ostentatious. What he did he did quietly, handsomely, completely; and he did much.[192]

XII. Statue of George Palmer 1891

There have been few days in Reading to match Wednesday 4 November 1891, which had been proclaimed a general holiday in the town. Among the various events, the statue of George Palmer was unveiled at 2pm in its original position in the middle of Broad Street.

Happily, the weather was fine that day, if rather dull, and so nothing prevented people from taking part in one or more of the several events organised. At noon the doors of the New Town Hall opened for those lucky enough to be ticket holders to witness the first event: the Presentation of the Freedom of the Borough to George Palmer. The well-known local organist, Mr Strickland, played a recital from 12.30 until 1pm, at which time the official procession entered the Hall, led by Daniel Heelas, Mayor, with Mr Palmer, to take their places on the platform.

The Town Clerk, Henry Day, opened proceedings by reading the minutes of the Town Council meeting of 27 October, admitting George Palmer to be an Honorary Freeman of the Borough, followed by the text of the inscription to be presented:

> Presented by the Corporation of Reading to George Palmer, Esq., J.P., of Reading, and Marlstone House, Berks, on his being admitted to the Honorary Freedom of the Borough, conferred by the Council of the Borough on the 28th day of October 1891.
>
> Dated this 4th day of November 1891[193]

George Palmer had arrived in Reading in 1841, 50 years before, and had made a remarkable impact on the town since that time. He had been born in Long Sutton, Somerset, on 18 January 1818 into a Quaker farming family. After early training with a relative in the milling and confectionery business, Palmer moved to Reading to join fellow Quaker, Thomas Huntley. Huntley was married to Palmer's first cousin, Jane Evans, and ran a biscuit bakery shop in London Street that had been opened by his father in 1822.[194] Together they formed the world-renowned partnership of biscuit manufacturers, Huntley & Palmer.

The firm opened up a large factory on King's Road in 1846, employing 41 men and boys. After Thomas Huntley, the senior of the two partners by 15 years, died aged 53 in March 1857,[195] George Palmer was joined by his brothers William Isaac and Samuel as partners of the firm, and so the company name was changed to Huntley & Palmers. The business grew to be the biggest employer in Reading, employing around 5,000 towards the end of the 19th century.[196]

Statue of George Palmer, now in Palmer Park

In 1850, George Palmer was elected onto the Reading Corporation [197] and remained a member until his retirement in November 1883.[198] He served as Mayor for a year from November 1857,[199] and was elected an alderman of the Borough in 1859.[200] He also served as one of the town's two MPs from 1878 to 1885, in the Liberal cause.[201]

However, it was his generosity and his active work for the town in many ways, and especially towards creating a more sanitary environment for the townspeople, that caused him to be seen as the leading Reading philanthropist and benefactor. In its obituary for George Palmer in 1897, the *Berkshire Chronicle*, generally no friend to Liberal politicians, wrote of him:

> Mr. Palmer took an active part in the various improvements which ... were completed in Reading, including the carrying out of the drainage scheme, the purchase of the waterworks, the removal of Middle Row, the removal of King's Road Corner, the alterations near the Town Hall, which were the prelude to the erection of the New Town Hall, Free Library and Museum, to which Mr. Palmer was a liberal contributor. Another important improvement was the removal of the fairs from the Forbury to a more suitable site, and the purchase of the Abbey Ruins and the open space there, and with the enclosure of the same. This deprived the children of the town of their sole means of recreation, but the Corporation then decided to purchase twelve acres of land in the King's Meadows as a recreation ground, and Mr. George Palmer, with conspicuous generosity, came forward and presented the adjoining fourteen acres to the town. Mr. Palmer also gave £500 to the re-erection of the almshouses in Castle Street, which were then in a state of decay...[202]

In the New Town Hall, that November day in 1891, the Mayor presented George Palmer with a silver ornamented casket that contained a medallion engraved with the inscription stating that the Freedom of the Borough was conferred on him. Then John A. Brain, Honorary Secretary of the Palmer Testimonial Committee, read out the address, which was bound in 'rich brown Morocco, padded,' with 'a sunk panel lined with purple velvet and bearing the Reading arms, engraved on a gilt plate.' The names of the 4,250 subscribers were to be appended to the document in due course.

Mr Palmer fittingly responded to the Mayor's speech regarding the presentation of the Freedom of the Borough, and the presentation of the testimonial. It was then time for the platform party to leave the New Town Hall and make their way the short distance to Broad Street for the unveiling of the statue.

Thousands of people had gathered around the statue, which was covered by a red cloth. It had been erected during the night by Messrs Wheeler, builders and masons, under the close direction of the sculptor, George Simonds, also the sculptor of the Maiwand Lion and Queen Victoria's statue.

The main party, escorted by the B (Reading) Troop of the Royal Berks Yeomanry Cavalry, took their places in the reserved area next to the statue. At 2pm, the Mayor, after a short speech, unveiled the statue, accompanied by 'hearty and enthusiastic cheering'.

The bronze statue is an unusual one, with Mr Palmer holding his hat and an umbrella. The *Berkshire Chronicle* reported:

> The artist has represented Mr. Palmer in an attitude in which he says he has often seen him. In his hand he holds his hat and umbrella, without which it is said no sensible Englishman ever goes out of doors. Mr. Palmer may be supposed to have taken off his hat before beginning to speak. In an artistic sense, the hat and umbrella are of use in giving strength and solidity to the lower part of the statue. The pedestal is of classic architectural design, and is executed in red Peterhead granite, polished throughout. The statue was cast at the works of Messrs. Singer of Frome, the head and hands having been cast by the waste wax process, and are left untouched by any chasing or subsequent operation after being taken from the mould...

> With regard to the artistic merits of the statue, we think it will grow with interest like the great lion and the statue of the Queen executed by the same artist; the more one looks at it the more one sees in it. It is undoubtedly a work of art, and viewed from the proper distance presents a striking likeness of Mr. Palmer, and will recall to future generations his familiar figure in the town. The proportions of the statue and pedestal are nicely adjusted. We are not sure that the position is the best that could have been chosen.[203]

The inscription on the front of the pedestal is:

> George Palmer J.P.
> Mayor of Reading
> 1857-8
> Member for the Borough
> 1878-1885

The inscription on the back:

> Erected
> by Public Subscription
> in recognition of
> the services and gifts of
> Mr. George Palmer
> to this Town
> 4 November
> 1891

The statue had been placed in the middle of Broad Street nearly opposite the junction with Minster Street, facing east. The Tramway Company had to alter the line of their rails so that the trams could pass either side. There were some who expressed the view that the statue would be better elsewhere (in the Forbury or Palmer Park), but the Broad Street location had been the unanimous choice of the committee involved and was a popular choice among Reading residents.

Following the unveiling of the statue, the bells of St Laurence's Church 'rang out in merry peal'. Then it was time for 'The Grand Procession' to the opening of Palmer Park. This was formed of 'cars' – we would call them floats now – manned by very many Reading and district organisations. Leading the way was the band of the Reading detachment of Volunteers. There were cyclists, Reading Athletics Club (two cars), then three football clubs – Reading, the Albion and the East Reading FC. Next was the Biscuit Factory Cricket Club ('one of the best cars'), followed by Reading Rowing Club then the committee of the Working Men's Regatta, the Swimming Club and the Waltonian Angling Society. Another band – the 3rd Battalion Royal Berks Regiment – came next, followed by the Foresters' Society, the Ancient Order of Shepherds, the Town Band, the Oddfellows, the Reading Friendly Society... In all there were about a hundred cars. The last 25 were the official procession: carriages carrying the officials and councillors, and finally one with the Mayor and his wife with Mr & Mrs George Palmer.

The estimate was that in all it took an hour for the procession to pass. Crowds lined the route from the statue to Palmer Park. George Palmer symbolically handed a silver key to the Mayor who, acknowledging the extremely generous gift of Mr Palmer in presenting the 49 acres of the park to the town, unlocked the gates to the park and declared it open to the public. The Mayor called for 'three times three' and the public responded heartily with their cheers.

The official procession then returned to the Town Hall by the direct route along King's Road, while the rest of the Grand Procession took a slightly longer route back. All along the routes flags and bunting were displayed from houses and from shops.

At 6pm, the pavilion and other buildings in Palmer Park were illuminated with 'ten thousand coloured lamps and Chinese lanterns'. This was immediately followed by a great display of fireworks in the park, orchestrated by the noted Mr James Pain of London. This was on a truly immense scale, including 'the wall of fire two hundred feet long with grand and novel effects, ... immense fire wheels, ... colossal fire portrait of Mr George Palmer, size covering an area of nine hundred square feet, surrounded by motto – "The town thanks you", worked out in large block letters.' Many thousands had assembled in the park and enjoyed this memorable display. The *Berkshire Chronicle* added: 'Fortunately this part of the day's proceedings passed off without any catastrophe occurring.'

In the evening there were free concerts in the New Town Hall (Reading Philharmonic Society concert) and in the Old Town Hall (Reading Orpheus Society concert), and a 'smoking concert' at the Assembly Rooms. The play *Mary Queen of Scots* was performed at 'the theatre'. Mr Palmer and his family made their way around all of these events, arriving amid cheers and staying for about 20 minutes or so before moving to the next venue.

Thus ended a day when 'not within the memory of the present generation have the inhabitants of Reading given themselves over to rejoicing as they did [on this day].'[204]

George Palmer died on 19 August 1897, aged 79, and was buried with his wife, who had died three years previously, in the Society of Friends' Burial Ground, Church Street.[205]

As traffic on Broad Street became motorised and ever busier, the statue began to be in the way in its central position near a junction. In 1928 the decision was taken to move it to Palmer Park.[206] Now that Broad Street is pedestrianised, it has been suggested that it is time to move this famous Reading man back to his more prominent position.[207] Personally, I agree.

THIS MARBLE TABLET
IS PLACED HERE BY
THE COUNCIL OF
THE BOROUGH OF READING
AS A MEMORIAL TO THE LATE
WILLIAM ISAAC PALMER J.
WHO DIED ON THE FOURTH OF
JANUARY ONE THOUSAND EIGHT
HUNDRED AND NINETY THREE
HE WAS A VERY MUNIFICENT
CONTRIBUTOR TO THE FUNDS FO[R]
THE ERECTION OF THE ADJACEN[T]
TOWN HALL AND FREE LIBRARY
AND MUSEUM BUILDINGS AND
TO HIM THE BOROUGH IS ALSO
LARGELY INDEBTED FOR THIS
ADDITION TO THOSE BUILDING[S]

WILLIAM FERGUSON,
                                    MAYOR.
HENRY DAY,
1897.   TOWN CLERK.

XIII. Memorial of William Isaac Palmer 1897

On Tuesday 19 October 1897, the memorial shown here was unveiled by Mrs Samuel Palmer. It is situated on the corner of the Art Gallery building, which was built in memory of William Isaac Palmer.

William Isaac Palmer was born at the Manor House, Elberton, Gloucestershire, on 31 May 1824. He followed in the footsteps of his older brothers George and Samuel by attending school in Sidcot, just off the Bath Road outside Bristol. Here he was 'under the guidance and teaching of a sturdy Quaker, Barton Dell.'[208] When he left school in 1838, William Isaac became an apprentice ironmonger with Joseph Huntley whose London Street shop was opposite his brother Thomas's biscuit bakery shop. Thomas was married to William Isaac's cousin, Jane Evans (daughter of William Isaac's mother's sister). In the latter part of the 1840s and into the 1850s, William Isaac worked as a commercial agent in Liverpool, and then joined Huntley & Palmer by 1855.[209]

In 1841 William Isaac's brother George, together with his sister and mother, had moved to Reading when George came into partnership with Thomas Huntley, forming Huntley & Palmer. William Isaac became a limited partner in the firm in October 1856, and a full partner in the renamed Huntley & Palmers on 19 October 1857.[210]

William Isaac Palmer became one of the best loved of Reading's residents. Following his death in 1893, the *Reading Mercury* wrote:

> An altogether unique figure has been removed from our midst, and even after three days have passed it is difficult to find words in which to express, however feebly, the sorrow felt, not only of the whole people of Reading and Berkshire, but of all to whom Mr. William I. Palmer was known, when on Wednesday the news of his unexpected death was made public. The announcement caused deep emotion in every circle, high and low, for Mr. Wm. Palmer was loved, nay revered, by persons of every rank in society, and of every religious and political creed.

> A man of strong and freely pronounced views, he never shrank from expressing his opinions with the frank and sometimes rugged honesty which was one of his chief characteristics. Those who were not intimately acquainted with the deceased often thought him abrupt, and at times even unsympathetic; but a very slight acquaintance turned his critics into warm admirers and a more intimate knowledge of his single-mindedness, of his unbounded personal charity, and of his warm-hearted sympathy

Memorial tablet to William Isaac Palmer. Corner of Blagrave Street and Valpy Street

with every movement which he believed to be for the general good, led those who really knew him to feel a chivalrous personal devotion towards him which was probably unparalleled in the history of this generation.[211]

The Town Hall complex in Reading consists of four buildings whose construction spans more than a hundred years, from 1786 to 1897. Prior to 1786, the Corporation met in a room above the one used by Reading School in the Hospitium Refectory building near St Laurence's Church. By 1786 this accommodation proved to be inadequate, and a new town hall was designed by Charles Poulton, an alderman of the Corporation, who strangely was not an architect but a cabinet maker. The new building consisted of a meeting chamber and an adjoining large hall. This latter room was filled on 17 August 1786 for the Town Hall's opening, with Handel's Messiah and one of the Coronation Anthems performed in the morning. In the evening, a 'Miscellaneous Concert' was followed at 10pm by a ball that lasted until 4 o'clock the next morning.[212] This part of the Town Hall complex, long known as the Old Town Hall, is now known as the Victoria Hall.

The next stage of building was completed in 1876 by the architect Alfred Waterhouse, noted for, amongst many other buildings, the Natural History Museum in Kensington. Waterhouse had moved to Reading in the late 1860s, building Foxhill House for his residence, now part of the University of Reading, in 1868.

The opening ceremony for the new municipal buildings took place at 4pm on Tuesday 6 June 1876, with the Lord Mayor of London as guest of honour.[213] The building contained a council chamber with a gallery along one side, a large committee room, several rooms for the Town Clerk and staff, rooms for the Borough Surveyor, other offices and storage. The building's main feature externally was the clock tower – '62 feet high to the top of the cornice, and to the finial about 100 ft.'[214] The Old Town Hall was hidden behind the Waterhouse façade of the new building.

The third part of the complex was opened almost six years later, in May 1882, and consisted of a new town hall, a free library, museum and schools for science and art. The impetus for the extension to the New Town Hall had come as early as February 1877, just eight months after the opening of the previous building. Thomas Bland Garland of Hillfields, Burghfield, offered the Council the extensive museum collection of his late uncle. In order to accommodate the collection, extra buildings were needed. This need soon developed into a larger project. In May 1877, at a 'Preliminary Meeting' in the Council Chambers:

> It was moved by Mr. Thomas Rogers, of Rosehill, Caversham, seconded by Mr. William Isaac Palmer, of Reading, and carried unanimously: —

> 'That in the opinion of this meeting, it is desirable in order to meet the wants of the large and rapidly increasing population of Reading and the surrounding neighbourhood, that there be erected in the Town of Reading,

a New Town Hall, capable of accommodating 2,000 persons, and Buildings suitable for a Public Free Library and Reading Rooms and Museum, and for Schools of Science and Art, including accommodation for the reception of the Museum Collection of the late Mr Horatio Bland...'[215]

In due course, architect Thomas Lainson of Brighton was engaged for the work. His initial proposals proved too expensive, and so a reduced plan was agreed costing the Corporation £10,000 with the remaining £34,000 covered by voluntary subscriptions. William Isaac Palmer was energetically involved throughout the project (as well as contributing £5,000 from his personal wealth, in addition to a similar donation from Huntley & Palmers). At the opening ceremony on Wednesday 31 May 1882, Alderman Blandy, in giving the main speech, said:

> ... the work could not have been carried on to the state in which the buildings were at the present time without the unflagging attention, the most minute consideration of details, the determination, the energy, and the liberality of one who, more than all, had devoted not only his means but his whole being to the advantage and improvement of the working classes of the town – he referred to Mr William Isaac Palmer. (Loud and prolonged cheers.)[216]

The Town Hall buildings were completed in 1897 by the addition of an art gallery and extensions to the library and museum, designed by William Roland Howell. This was built on the site formerly occupied by the County Court offices at the corner of Valpy Street and Blagrave Street, the land being given by George Palmer and Samuel Palmer, with the building being erected in memory of their late brother William Isaac Palmer.

At the opening of the art gallery on Tuesday 19 October 1897, the Mayor of Reading, William Ferguson, called it 'the completion of a work very near to the heart of... Mr William Isaac Palmer, whose princely liberality and indefatigable labours contributed so much both to the provision of the adjoining Free Public Library and Museum, and other public buildings, and also to the success of the work carried on therein.'[217]

William Isaac had died on 4 January 1893, aged 68, after a short illness. The *Reading Mercury* called him 'a keen man of business, a clever mechanician, an able magistrate, a good landlord and a true friend ... one of the greatest philanthropists of the day.'[218]

Unfortunately, George Palmer did not live to see the completion of the art gallery as he died two months before the opening in October 1897. The third brother, Samuel, was unable to be present at the opening due to his poor health. Therefore, Samuel's wife, Mary, was the one who, using the special solid silver key, unlocked the entrance doors of the art gallery and declared the building open. Their son, Samuel Ernest Palmer, responded to the Mayor's vote of thanks on behalf of his parents.

The art gallery contained paintings to the value of £1,000 from William Isaac Palmer's collection[219] and the copy of the Bayeux Tapestry, donated by Arthur Hill.[220] In addition, there were a few other pieces in the gallery, including a cast of Dionysius by George Simonds, and some portraits that had been loaned. The whole had been supplemented by a 'most excellent loan from South Kensington'.[221]

The inscription on the memorial tablet shown at the beginning of this chapter says:

> This Marble Tablet is placed here by
> the Council of the Borough of Reading
> as a Memorial to the late William Isaac Palmer J.P.
> who died on the fourth of January 1893.
> He was a very munificent contributor to the funds for
> the erection of the adjacent Town Hall and Free Library
> and Museum buildings and to him the borough is also
> largely indebted for this addition to those buildings.
> William Ferguson Mayor
> Henry Day Town Clerk
> 1897

The tablet was not approved of by all. The *Reading Observer* editorial some weeks before the opening ceremony, when the memorial was first erected, declaimed: 'Who is responsible for the Tablet which has recently been placed on the wall of the new Reading Art Gallery?' The first complaint was that the material being 'black grained marble' was so 'grained' that the inscription could not be read. (The passer by now would have a different complaint: the marble is completely white, and the writing is hard to make out.) It continued with the scathing comment regarding the wording: 'We presume that [the inscription] must be taken as a specimen of English composition; but what English!' It then considered it unnecessary for the inscription to state that it is made of marble, complained about the use of the present tense 'is placed here,' and fulminated that it should be a memorial *of* rather than *to* the late William Isaac Palmer. However, its most serious complaint was over William Isaac's role as described by the tablet:

> We are under the impression that the site of the Art Gallery was the gift of Messrs. GEORGE and SAMUEL PALMER (in order to carry out the expressed intention of their late brother), and that the building itself was erected at the cost of the town. How then can this be reconciled with the statement that 'to him' (Mr. W. I. Palmer) 'the Borough is also largely indebted for this addition' (that is the marble Tablet) 'to these buildings.'[222]

The general view of the memorial, however, was not the same as that of the *Reading Observer* editorial. The *Berkshire Chronicle* states that 'the tablet is of St Ann's marble, enclosed in a handsome frame of the same marble, the inscription being beautifully cut and richly gilded. The whole of the work was executed at Fitt's Monumental Works, London Road.'[223]

Above the memorial there is a series of four friezes by Reading-born sculptor William Charles May. The first, leftmost, frieze represents 'Ancient Britons' and has a blacksmith at his anvil with his little daughter behind, a hunter/warrior and his bulldog and a man making flint implements, with a druid looking on. The subject of the second frieze panel is 'Roman Arts and Industries', showing Roman blacksmiths, potters and a sculptor. The third panel illustrates 'Literature' with Homer surrounded by famous figures including Charles Dickens and Chaucer. The fourth and final panel depicts 'Science', with a medley of inventors and inventions, including Thomas Edison and explorer Fridtjof Nansen (who had recently mounted an expedition to the North Pole).

There is one other frieze, also by William Charles May, showing King Henry I laying the foundation stone of Reading Abbey in 1121. Above this frieze is a statue of Queen Victoria, produced in 1882 (five years before the Jubilee statue nearby), which was paid for by William Isaac Palmer.

There is another memorial to William Isaac Palmer in the town centre: West Street Hall has 'W. I. Palmer Memorial Hall' emblazoned on its front. This hall was built in 1861 and was formally opened by Alderman George Palmer at a public meeting at 8pm on 21 August that year.[224]

The hall, measuring 54 feet by 35½ feet, could hold 400–500 persons. At the west end there was a semi-circular platform, with a domed roof above to project the speaker's voice. There were several other rooms, including a committee room, and entrances on West Street and Friars Place. Its design was freely given by William Woodman. The building cost £1,200, raised by share capital and subscriptions.[225]

Both William Isaac and George Palmer were closely involved in the project to build West Street Hall from start to completion. At the opening, William Isaac Palmer described the running of the hall:

> The Temperance Society occupied the whole of the place as tenants, at a moderate rent, except that part which the School of Art held, but they had not a smoking room, as was the case during the existence of the Working Men's Club, and neither were intoxicating drinks sold; coffee, &c., were, however, supplied. They had a reading room supplied with newspapers, periodicals, &c., a library, consisting of about 1,000 books, &c., and the terms were fixed at as low a rate as possible. The hall would be let for public purposes to those who required it, at moderate charges...[226]

The hall was renovated in 1887 and William Isaac Palmer funded a new front to the building (designed by Spencer Slingsby Stallwood) in commemoration of the jubilee of the Reading Temperance Society, of which William Isaac was President.[227] He remained President of the Society until he died in 1893.

In April 1899 the West Street Hall was closed for a complete remodelling, which included removal of the façade except for the ornate doorway, and was opened the following year as the 'W. I. Palmer Memorial Building' on Wednesday 29 June 1900 by Samuel Ernest Palmer, son of William Isaac's brother Samuel.[228]

XIV. Martin Hope Sutton Memorial 1902

On Thursday 27 November 1902, the Martin Hope Sutton Memorial Hall on Sackville Street, off Greyfriars Road, was officially opened. The Hall, built by subscription and attached to Greyfriars Church, carries the name of one of Reading's most famous sons.

The firm of Sutton & Sons, appointed by Royal Warrant to be Seed Merchants to the Queen in 1884, had its beginnings in a small shop – the 'House of Sutton' – at 13 King Street. This was opened in 1806 by John Sutton, Martin Hope Sutton's father.

John's business as a corn factor and miller prospered for the first few years as the price of corn was high because of the war against Napoleon. He was then hit in 1814 by a combination of peace and the failure of the corn harvest. As if that was not enough, a further blow came when his bank, Marsh & Deane of Reading, folded in January 1815. John owed them nearly £1,000 and his debt was called in by the Commissioners of Bankruptcy who had come in to deal with the bank's failure.[229]

John was able to come to an agreement with the Commissioners, which allowed him to continue to trade, although his finances were extremely straitened for a considerable time.

On 14 March that difficult year, John's wife Sarah gave birth to their second son and they gave him the middle name of Hope 'as an expression of faith that a good future was in store for him.'[230]

A great deal is known about Martin Hope because he kept a wealth of personal papers, including three diaries (personal, religious and business), letters and many pages of notes.

Martin Hope attended a boys' day school in the early 1820s run by Joseph Huntley. Huntley opened his biscuit and cake shop in London Street in 1822, although he must have kept the school going too as Martin Hope attended until 1825. After Huntley's, he attended Thomas Greathead's academy in Castle Street, until he needed to leave school to assist his father, who had begun to suffer from poor health.[231]

Martin Hope Sutton joined his father's company when he was 12. After two years' work in the granaries, he moved to the counting house. It was here that he began to analyse the finances of the business and plan to make it more profitable. He decided that the corn and flour side of the firm could not improve but became interested in the agricultural seeds, which were at the time a side-line.

Martin Hope believed that selling seeds could become more profitable and started looking into the possibilities. His father did not approve and Martin Hope had to do all his studying and research in his own time. Aged 16, he opened an account with a London wholesale seed firm (in his father's name as he was still a minor). He also began the habit of taking long walks of 20 miles or so to read books on botany and to visit nurseries.

In order to improve his father's business, Martin Hope began to advertise. The first newspaper advertisement ran in the *Reading Mercury* in December 1832:

> **THE GENUINE**
> **EARLY WHITE WARWICK PEAS**
> Grown by Mr. R. Webb;
> May now be had in any Quantity, at Five
> Shillings per Gallon, of
> **JOHN SUTTON, SEEDSMAN &C.**
> **13 KING-STREET, READING**[232]

He also produced a printed broadsheet, an early style of catalogue. His father agreed to provide him with an area of ground in the Forbury for him to dig, sow and produce his plants and seeds. Unfortunately, Martin Hope did not possess a strong constitution and his work in the garden at all hours and in all conditions soon led to his doctor despairing of his life unless he changed his ways. As a result, Martin Hope was sent to work for F. Hawkes & Sons, estate agents, auctioneers and surveyors, of West Street. However, this proved to be much less to Martin Hope's liking and he soon returned to the seed business.

He became an active member of the Reading Horticultural Society. This Society had been formed at a meeting at the Reading Town Hall on 17 December 1833 and had held its first show on 21 May the following year.[233] Martin Hope regularly took part in their shows both as a judge and as an exhibitor.

The Memorial Plaque and Hall – Greyfriars Church behind

In 1836, when Martin Hope was 21, his father made him a partner in the firm and the name of the business changed to John Sutton & Son. Son became Sons when John's third son, Alfred, became a partner in 1843. In January 1837, the business moved into larger premises at 7 & 8 Market Place (although the King Street shop continued to be used until September that year). The new shop was in a prime position, looking out at the agricultural market held in Market Place every Saturday.

The growing importance to the business of selling seed can be gauged from the fact that seed went from 2 per cent to 42 per cent of the firm's stocks between 1832 and 1839.[234]

Martin Hope was a fervent Royalist, who made the most of the opportunity of Queen Victoria's coronation day on 28 June 1838 to be fully involved. As part of the festivities a huge banquet was held in Market Place for over 2,000 children from the local Charity Schools and Sunday Schools. The tables were 'very handsomely ornamented with flowers, by the Messrs. Suttons, who also exhibited in the front of their house [i.e. shop], the royal initials executed in wreaths.'[235] Martin Hope himself presided at one of the tables 'carving the roast beef and dishing out the plum pudding.'[236]

1840 was the year that the business was transformed from a small provincial town's concern to a national, then international business. First, with the advent of the penny post on 10 January, Sutton & Sons became one of the first mail order businesses in the world. Then on 30 March, the Great Western Railway reached Reading and Martin Hope was there to see the first train depart – and to sell flower seeds at the station![237]

In the same year, Martin Hope established the first laboratory to test seeds for purity and germination. As a consequence, Sutton & Sons became known for the quality of their seeds at a time when many suppliers mixed their seed with old or dead seed to reduce costs and increase profits. As the business expanded, it also became known for how well it treated its workforce.

Eventually the company occupied six acres of land behind the Sutton & Sons Market Place shop front, with many buildings devoted to storage and mail order despatch, sending seeds across the world. In 1873 the shop was given a new frontage, with bold lettering proudly proclaiming, 'Sutton & Sons, Royal Berkshire Seed Establishment, Seedsmen to the Queen.'

Martin Hope was frequently summoned by Queen Victoria to advise on the gardens at Osborne on the Isle of Wight and at Windsor Castle. He also hosted a visit by the Prince of Wales (the future King Edward VII) to the Sutton seed trial grounds at London Road, Earley, in 1882.[238]

Martin Hope Sutton married Charlotte Trendell, the daughter of a local goldsmith of Minster Street, on 6 February 1844 at St Mary's Church.[239] Charlotte was an Evangelical Christian, and this had a profound effect on Martin Hope, who became far more serious about religion. Sadly, their two children died in infancy and Charlotte herself died of consumption in 1846, aged just 28.[240]

Martin Hope married again, on 19 September 1848 at St Laurence's Church, to Sophia Woodhead Warwick. By 1865 they had 9 children, 4 girls and 5 boys. The family moved to Cintra Lodge in 1857, described for sale as:

> ...the very handsome and modern FREEHOLD VILLA RESIDENCE called 'CINTRA LODGE,' delightfully situated at Whitley Hill, within half a mile of the town of Reading, and one mile from the Great Western, South-Eastern and South-Western Railway Stations. The house, which is substantially built in the Italian style of architecture, and has been erected about six years, contains a good entrance hall, capital dining room; handsome drawing room, communicating with an elegant conservatory, and a balcony with verandah to the south, three principal bed rooms, dressing room, two small rooms in the tower, a day and a night nursery, housekeeper's sitting room and bed room, a large breakfast room, kitchen, scullery, china closet, wine cellar, butler's pantry, larder, dairy, coal cellar, water closets, two coach houses, stable, harness room, loft and two men-servants' rooms. There is a large walled-in GARDEN, well planted, with LAWN in front; and the whole including the site of the buildings, contains, by estimation, about an acre and a quarter (more or less). There is a good supply of water.[241]

Although he kept himself well informed of political issues, he never involved himself in political or civic life. His father had been a Freemason, but Martin Hope did not belong to that organisation.[242] Rather he belonged to a large number of Christian organisations, including the Young Men's Christian Association, Church Pastoral Aid Society, British and Foreign Bible Society, Church Missionary Society, and many more.[243]

In December 1863 Greyfriars Church, which had been restored after being the town's Bridewell, or prison, was re-consecrated as a parish church and from thenceforth followed a strong Evangelical Christian tradition. This suited Martin Hope, and he and his family became members of the congregation.[244] His daughter Laura married the second vicar of Greyfriars, Rev Seymour Henry Soole, in 1876.

Martin Hope retired from the business in 1888, on the same day as his brother Alfred, leaving it in the hands of his sons, Martin John Sutton (see the next chapter) and Arthur Warwick Sutton. It was said that Martin Hope continued to interfere in the running of the company, much to the annoyance of his sons![245]

Martin Hope Sutton died, aged 86, on 4 October 1901. His obituary in The Times described his many philanthropic acts, especially those connected with church and missionary charities. The *Reading Mercury* wrote that 'Mr. Sutton was indeed imbued, nay saturated, with the spirit of true religion – ever seeking the good of his fellow man before his own, ever striving to do good in his generation.'[246]

The town flags were flown at half-mast on the day of his funeral, with shop shutters down and curtains drawn at private houses. These were visible signs of 'a genuine and widely felt sorrow at the decease of one of the founders of Reading's greatness.' Thousands silently lined the route to Greyfriars Church and then, later on, to the cemetery. The cortège was over a mile long with more than 80 carriages.[247]

With Martin Hope Sutton's passing came the desire to mark his life with a memorial. The Martin Hope Sutton Memorial Hall subscription list opened in March 1902, and soon raised sufficient money to cover the £750 costs of the building.[248]

The Hall, designed by architects Ravenscroft, Son, & Morris of the Forbury, was officially opened at 3.30pm on Thursday 27 November 1902 by Martin Hope's son-in-law, the vicar of Greyfriars, Rev Seymour Henry Soole. The room was 34 feet long by 20 feet wide with an entrance lobby on the front, at the Sackville Street entrance, and lavatories at the rear. Its facing of flint and stone was designed to match the church. The main contractors were Messrs Wheeler of Caversham Road, and Messrs Callas, Sons & May installed the electric lighting and the hot water heating system.[249] Both the Wheeler and the Callas families were Greyfriars Church members.

Inside Greyfriars Church there is a second memorial to Martin Hope Sutton, on the south wall in the south transept. This was paid for and erected by Martin Hope's nine children.

XV. Statue of King Edward VII 1902

In pouring rain on Wednesday 3 December 1902, Prince Christian of Schleswig-Holstein, the King's brother-in-law, unveiled the first statue of His Majesty King Edward VII to be erected.[250] The statue was given to the town by Mr Martin John Sutton, as a commemoration of the coronation and in memory of his father Martin Hope Sutton who had died the previous year. The statue is now Grade II Listed.[251]

On 22 January 1901, Queen Victoria died aged 81 at Osborne House, her retreat on the Isle of Wight. Her eldest son, Albert Edward, who became King Edward VII, was in his 60th year when he came to the throne. Unlike Victoria, who never visited Reading, Edward was no stranger to the town, having visited it on four occasions when he was Prince of Wales, including visits to Sutton & Sons in 1882 and 1890.[252]

In March 1902, a large gathering met in the Small Town Hall to consider how the town should mark the coronation of the King and of Queen Alexandra on 26 June. At the meeting the Mayor, Mr A. H. Bull, read out a letter from Martin John Sutton:

> Henley Park, Oxon
> March 18th, 1902
>
> To the Worshipful the Mayor of Reading.
>
> Dear Mr Mayor,—Having heard with regret that there will be no public funds available for the erection of any permanent memorial in connection with the commemoration by Reading of their Majesties' Coronation, and feeling that some memento of the loyal and patriotic sentiments called forth by that auspicious event in this chief town of the Royal County should exist for all future time, I have the honour to inform you as Chief Magistrate that I propose to ask the Borough of Reading to accept a statue of His Majesty King Edward VII in his Coronation robes, as a fitting complement to the statue of Queen Victoria, erected on the occasion of the Jubilee.
>
> As I know my late father, who received during his long life many personal favours from the Royal Family, would have wished to give the statue himself, I desire to associate his name with my gift to the town he loved so well.
>
> I am, dear Mr Mayor, yours very truly,
>
> MARTIN J. SUTTON
>
> P.S.—It would be my wish that on one side of the pedestal of the statue a tablet should be affixed recording in detail the Coronation ceremonies and festivities celebrated in Reading under your Mayoralty.— M.J.S.[253]

The commission for the statue went to Mr George Edward Wade, of The Avenue, Fulham Road, London, who had a reputation for producing faithful portraits in stone. The *Oxford Dictionary of National Biography* says of him:

> The popularity of Wade's sculpture was probably due not only to the fact that it was always comprehensible but that it was both ennobling and restrained in equal measure. In portraiture he obtained at the same time a good likeness, much appreciated by the sitters and their families, and, in these works and in his more fanciful subjects, he engendered feelings of respect and admiration. It might be argued by some that his approach was too prosaic, but it would perhaps be more true to say that he cloaked classical ideals in the trappings of his own environment.[254]

As 26 June drew closer, many committees consisting of a multitude of volunteers prepared for the two days of celebrations planned. A celebratory banquet was held on Monday evening, 23 June by the Reading & District Licensed Trade, with the Mayor presiding.[255] Concern was expressed about reports that the King was not in good health, but the hope was that all he needed was a good rest before the coronation due to take place on Thursday.

However, shortly after midday on the following day it was announced that the King's condition had deteriorated and that he would need an urgent operation. As a consequence, the coronation was postponed.[256]

In Reading, at a hurriedly convened meeting of the coronation committees, it was decided that all festivities should be called off. Not everyone was happy about this, leading some to be vociferous in their complaints that other local towns were going ahead with their plans and so, they believed, should Reading. The *Berkshire Chronicle*, however, supported the decision to cancel:

> ...the meeting was practically [unanimous]... that Reading... did not intend to indulge in festivities while the King was lying in a critical state at Buckingham Palace. With that decision we most cordially agree.

> Some of the statements which have been made show how little serious thought has been given to the matter by these amateur critics. Apart from the question of good taste, it has been forgotten that such festivities as the children's fete and the old folks' dinner would be practically impossible except the days for these rejoicings were kept as Bank Holidays. In Reading the tradesmen sensibly resolved to open their business premises on Thursday and Friday; and in very few cases in the town was business suspended.[257]

Following the King's recovery, it was announced that the new date for the coronation would be Saturday 9 August, with a public holiday declared for that

King Edward VII

day. The events in Reading were commemorated, as Martin John Sutton had desired, on a plaque on the back of the King's statue. Beneath the Town Arms, the inscription states:

Coronation
of
His Majesty King Edward VII
1902.

Record of the
Commemorative Celebrations
and Public Rejoicings held
in the County Borough of Reading.

Dinner to 2000 Aged Poor Persons.
Tea to 14,500 School Children.

Special Services at
Churches and Chapels.
Procession of the Town Council,
and of Oddfellows, Foresters, and
other Benefit and Friendly Societies;
Trade, Florally Decorated, Emblematic,
and Historical Cars, and
Decorated Carriages, including
Automobiles and Cycles.
Aquatic Sports, Amateur & Non-Amateur
and Old English Sports.
Water Carnival with procession of
illuminated and decorated boats
and steam launches.
Royal Salute.
Planting commemoration tree in the
Forbury Pleasure Grounds
by the Mayoress.
Illuminated Promenade Concerts.
Torchlight Procession attended by the
Mayor and by the Chairmen and
Secretaries of the Coronation Committees.
Distribution of Medals and Coronation
Pictures by the Mayor & the Mayoress.

Alfred Holland Bull J.P. Mayor.
Henry Day, Town Clerk

The statue of the King was not ready by the coronation date. The pedestal was put in place in late November 1902 at the western end of Blagrave Street, opposite the railway station, where it still stands. The statue itself was erected on Monday 1 December ready for the unveiling ceremony two days later.[258]

In late September 1902 the Council had decided to award Mr Martin John Sutton JP and Alderman George William Palmer JP, MP, the Freedom of the Borough.[259] It had been decided that the presentations should take place on the same day as the unveiling of the King's statue – Wednesday 3 December.

On the day, His Royal Highness Frederick Christian Charles Augustus, Prince Christian of Schleswig-Holstein, KG, GCB, GCVO, PC, arrived by train from Paddington at 11.40. His carriage to the Town Hall was accompanied by an escort from the Berkshire Yeomanry. In the Council chamber the Mayor read a loyal address to the King and of welcome to the Prince.

Then the Prince, Mayor and members of the Council processed to the Large Town Hall for the ceremony of presentation of the Freedom of the Borough. The Mayor read the citation for Mr Palmer first:

> That this Council having regard to the eminent services rendered to this Borough by George William Palmer, Esquire, J.P., M.P., of Reading, and of Marlston House, Berks, as the Representative of this Borough in Parliament for upwards of seven years, as Member of the Council of the Borough for twenty years, in the course of which period he held the Office of Mayor; as a large contributor to the educational and benevolent Institutions of the Borough; and as a promoter of the commercial prosperity of the Borough, do hereby ... confer upon the said George William Palmer, Esquire, the Honorary Freedom of the Borough of Reading.[260]

The Mayor then read the second citation:

> That Martin John Sutton, Esquire, J.P., of Reading and of Henley Park, in the County of Oxford, having distinguished himself in promoting the interests of Agriculture in the Country, this Council, having regard thereto, to Mr Sutton's life-long work in furtherance of the commercial prosperity of the Borough and in the support of various benevolent Institutions, especially those having for their object the welfare of young men; and to his generous gift to the Corporation of a Statue of His Majesty King Edward the Seventh as a permanent Memorial of the Coronation of His Majesty, do hereby in pursuance of the Honorary Freedom of Boroughs Act, 1885, confer upon the said Martin John Sutton, Esquire, the Honorary Freedom of the Borough of Reading.[261]

The two men thus honoured were, as the Mayor stated, both promoters of the 'commercial prosperity of the Borough'. George William Palmer was the eldest son of George Palmer (see Chapter XII) and involved in the management of Huntley & Palmers all his working life. He became Chairman of the company in 1904.

Martin John Sutton was the eldest son of Martin Hope Sutton (see Chapter XIV) and became a partner in Sutton & Sons at 21, and then head of the firm in 1887. Like his father, he was a great believer in agricultural research. A book he wrote in 1886, *Permanent and Temporary Pastures* (dedicated, incidentally, to HRH Albert Edward, Prince of Wales), became the standard work on the subject and was reprinted many times. He was chosen to be Mayor of Reading in 1904 despite not being a councillor.[262]

After the presentations of the Freedom of the Borough, it was time for the official procession on foot to the site of the statue, led by Mr George E. Wade, the sculptor. In spite of the inclement weather, a large crowd had gathered to see the unveiling by Prince Christian. As the statue was revealed, there was loud cheering, followed by the singing of the National Anthem. A banquet lunch followed, in the Corn Exchange, accompanied by the usual speeches and toasts. Prince Christian travelled back to London on the 4.03 train, bringing a memorable day for all concerned to a close.

The statue:

> which is of bronze, and is nine feet in height, is one for which the King himself gave sittings. His Majesty is represented in the uniform of a Field Marshall, wearing the Parliamentary robe and holding the Sceptre in the right hand and Orb in the left. It faces north, that is towards the Great Western Railway Station. The statue stands on a red granite pedestal 12 feet high. It is not polished, but fine axed. There are two large bronze panels bearing the names and titles of His Majesty, together with the name of the donor of the statue and also an account of the celebrations in Reading commemorative of the King's Coronation. The panel in front bears the shield with the Royal Arms and heraldic scroll work and on the back panel are the Reading Arms. Both the statue and panels are cast in a golden bronze.[263]

The panel on the front bears the following inscription:

> His Majesty Edward VII
> King of Great Britain
> and Ireland and of
> the British Dominions beyond the Seas
> Emperor of India.
>
> This Statue was presented to the Town of Reading by
> Martin John Sutton
> eldest son of the late Martin Hope Sutton
> who for 86 years was a resident in this Borough.

XVI. Dr Valpy Memorial Plaque 1904

In September 1904, just a few weeks before the 150th anniversary of his birth, a plaque was attached to the wall of the Reading Art Gallery, in Valpy Street, to commemorate the most notable Head Master of Reading School.

Richard Valpy was born in St John's parish, Jersey, on 7 December 1754. His school days from age 10 were spent away from home, at Valognes in Normandy, then at grammar schools in Southampton and Guildford. His first book, *Poetical Blossoms; Or, a Collection of Poems, Odes, and Translations, by a Young Gentleman of the Royal Grammar School, Guildford*, was published by subscription in 1772.

He matriculated at Pembroke College, Oxford, in April 1773, having been awarded one of Jersey's Bishop Morley Scholarships. He received his degree in 1776 and then took Holy Orders. However, he did not take up a curacy, but rather became Under-Master at Bury St Edmund's School. In 1778 he married Martha Cornelius in Jersey and they were blessed with a daughter in the following year. Martha sadly died aged just 22 in January 1781.[264]

Soon after, while travelling to Jersey, Valpy met former Reading School Head Master, Rev John Spicer, who told him that the Mastership of Reading School was vacant and advised him to apply for it.[265] Valpy followed this advice and on 18 September 1781 Reading Corporation appointed him to be Head Master of Reading School. He is often quoted as becoming Head Master at age 27, but in fact he celebrated his 27th birthday after nearly a term in charge of the school.

In the following year, Valpy married again, to Miss Mary Benwell of Caversham.[266] This union was blessed with six sons and five daughters – all except one daughter surviving to adulthood – and lasted until Mary's death in June 1816. Upon her death, newspapers reported:

> Such was the anxious attention of this amiable lady towards the numerous young gentlemen educated at the Doctor's eminent seminary, that none left it but regarded her as a parent and will ever continue to cherish the memory of their earliest and most affectionate friend.[267]

Reading School was at something of a low ebb when Valpy arrived in September 1781, it being described as 'in a reduced state.'[268] The Master's House had been built in 1731 by Haviland Hiley (Head Master 1716–1750) and accommodated twenty boarders. Valpy initially rented this house, but was able to raise sufficient funds, mostly through the former pupils of the school, to purchase it. Over time, he extended the house by several extra rooms, including a library.

Meanwhile, something had to be done about the schoolroom accommodation. For over 200 years the schoolroom had been the ground floor of the former Abbey Hospitium building, with the upper floor used by the Corporation as the Town Hall. Valpy set about trying to improve the situation.

THIS TABLET RECALLS TO MEMORY
THE REVD RICHARD VALPY, D.D.
WHO FOR NEARLY 50 YEARS (1781-1830) WAS
HEAD MASTER OF READING SCHOOL
BORN IN JERSEY DECEMBER 7TH 1754
DIED IN KENSINGTON MARCH 28 1836
THE OLD SCHOOL HOUSE OCCUPIED THIS SITE

First, however, things got worse. In 1786 the new Town Hall was completed around the Hospitium site. Not only was the schoolroom not part of the improvements, but it also suffered a reduction in its light and an increase in noise due to the elasticity of the new floor above.

In spite of his efforts, Valpy could not get the Corporation to take any action, so he took matters into his own hands. He purchased some land and paid for a new schoolroom to be erected – 'a large and commodious room, fifty-two feet in length', erected in 1790. The ground floor of the Hospitium was converted into more boarding accommodation.[269]

At this time, the Forbury was much larger than the present Forbury Gardens. It included the large area now occupied by Valpy Street, including the Hospitium and a large area to the north. Both the Master's House and the new schoolroom faced into the open area of the Forbury, the latter built approximately where the art gallery extends along Valpy Street (as stated on the plaque shown opposite).

The school's playground was actually part of the public area of the Forbury. Reading School boys and town boys often came into conflict over the space. The latter would make a point of playing cricket in the area, so the former spiked the ground with 'stout pegs which stood a little above the surface, but so as not to attract attention; this had the effect of tripping up those who ventured to play there.'[270]

The reputation of the school grew under Valpy, who became Dr Valpy with the award of a doctorate in Divinity in 1792. He had also become rector of Stradishall in Suffolk in 1787, although he cannot often have been present there.

The number of students at the school increased, peaking at 119 in 1792. Success was not maintained, however, and by the time Dr Valpy retired in 1830 there were just 65.[271] Valpy's successor was his son Francis, who is often incorrectly charged with reducing the numbers of students from 200 to 30,

Dr Valpy memorial plaque

This tablet recalls to memory
The Revd Richard Valpy, D.D.
who for nearly 50 years (1781–1830) was
Head Master of Reading School.
Born in Jersey December 7th 1754
Died at Kensington March 28th 1836.

The Old School House occupied this site.

rather than the more modest fall of 65 to 30.[272]

Dr Valpy was a larger-than-life character. In spite of being famously known as a 'mighty flogger', he was admired, even loved, by his students. One of these, Rev Benjamin Bradney Bockett, under the pseudonym Oliver Oldfellow, wrote fondly and wittily of school life under Dr Valpy (albeit with disguised names) in *Our School: or Scraps and Scrapes in Schoolboy Life*, giving Valpy the name Dr Duodecimus Wackerbach.[273]

Throughout his career, Valpy was a prolific author of school books. His first major work was *The Elements of the Latin Language* OR *An Introduction to the Latin Grammar in a New, Easy and Concise Method*, published at the end of April 1782. His most notable book, published in early 1813, was generally known as the *Greek Delectus* and used by generations of school pupils.[274]

Valpy was also something of a showman. Both at the school's annual Speech Day and at the triennial Visitation Day by Oxford University, the school put on Greek plays and plays by Shakespeare. The latter were his own versions and were often published. He wrote of the alterations to the two parts of Henry IV:

> When the First part of King Henry the Fourth was played at Reading School, it was sufficient to curtail some tedious pages, and to omit some exceptional expressions. In the Second Part it was absolutely necessary to do more. This play in the original is disfigured not only with indelicate speeches, but with characters that cannot now be tolerated on a public theatre.[275]

When Valpy retired after 49 years as Head Master of Reading School, he went to live in his rectory in Stradishall, remaining rector there for the rest of his life. He died on 28 March 1836, aged 81, at his son's house in Kensington, London, having fallen and broken his leg.[276] His mausoleum in Kensal Green Cemetery is a Grade II Listed monument.[277]

A group of old boys (the *Berkshire Chronicle* mentions Mr Baron Bolland and Serjeants Merewether and Thomas Noon Talfourd) commissioned the sculptor Samuel Nixon to carve a life-sized statue of Dr Valpy, using stone from the quarry of Roche Abbey, Yorkshire.[278] The sculptor had to create the likeness of his subject, whom he had never met, from a bust by Westmacott and an 1801 portrait by Opie (a copy of which now hangs in Big School, Reading School's hall). When the statue arrived in the town, ready to be installed in St Laurence's Church, opinion given by the Valpy family and those who knew Dr Valpy was that the likeness was a good one.[279]

The statue was installed in the church on Friday 14 December 1838. It is quite difficult to see the detail of the statue as it is elevated several feet above a large inscription plaque, which is itself above a doorway in the south-west corner of the church. The long Latin inscription was written by the Rev Dr Major, a former Reading School pupil under Dr Valpy, and by this time Head Master of King's College School, London.[280]

The next memorial to Dr Valpy in Reading was considered in 1878:

The [Survey] Committee again met on the 26th ult. [April] when a letter was read from Messrs W. and J. T. Brown, notifying Mr J. H. Blagrave's consent to the proposal of the committee that the new road from Blagrave-street to the Forbury should be called Valpy-street.[281]

It was very fitting that this new road be called Valpy Street. Not only was it a suitable way for the town to remember him, but also the location chosen was completely apt as it was so near the site of Reading School until its move into its new buildings designed by Alfred Waterhouse off Erleigh Road.

The final memorial to Valpy was the one shown at the beginning of the chapter. At a meeting of the Finance and General Purposes Committee of Reading Town Council on Thursday 27 February 1902 the committee considered the following letter from Mr J. J. Cooper:

'At the request of Mr Edward Valpy, of New York, U.S.A., a descendant of Dr Richard Valpy, the famous Head Master of Reading School (1781–1830), I beg to make application to the Town Council through your Worship as follows:– I ask permission to insert, at Mr Valpy's cost, in the external wall of the Art Gallery, in Valpy-street, a tablet briefly recording Dr Valpy's long and honourable connection with Reading and its school. After consulting Mr William Ravenscroft, F.S.A., and examining with him the old plan of that part of the town, I find that the Art Gallery occupies part of the site of the old school-house, so that its outer wall would be the most appropriate place in which to insert such a tablet. Should the Council assent to Mr Valpy's request thus made through me, I shall be happy to submit particulars to anyone you may depute to act on your behalf.'

The Committee having considered the matter resolved that the spot for the tablet be fixed by the Mayor, the Chairman of the Committee and Ald. Blandy, that the Corporation undertake no responsibility for the maintenance of the tablet and that it be removable by the Corporation at any time when they may deem it necessary to remove it.[282]

It took until September 1904 for the tablet actually to be placed on the wall in Valpy Street.[283] It remains on the wall of the Art Gallery, perhaps slightly higher than most people's gaze, but testimony to one who certainly made his mark on the town.

XVII. King Henry I Memorial Cross 1909

The impressive memorial to King Henry I, the founder of Reading Abbey, was a gift to the town by Dr Jamieson B. Hurry. It stands within the footprint of the old Abbey Church. The memorial was unveiled on Friday 18 June 1909, but the public were not admitted so that there could be no disruption from 'militant suffragettes'.

Reading was probably an important place before the founding of the Abbey in 1121.[284] Straddling the river Kennet and not far from the Thames, there was a good-sized settlement described 35 years earlier in the Domesday Book.[285] It had belonged to the King since at least the days of Edward the Confessor, which might have meant that it was used as a centre for administration and, as a natural consequence, tax collection across the Hundred of Reading.[286]

However, without doubt, what put Reading on the map was the decision by Henry I Beauclerc to found an Abbey on the site of the Saxon burgh. William of Malmesbury wrote that Henry 'built this monastery between the rivers Kennet and Thames in a spot calculated for the reception of almost all who might have occasion to travel to the more populous cities of England.'[287]

A relatively recent idea suggests that Henry decided to found the Abbey as a result of losing his son and heir William in the wreck of the White Ship in November 1120, but the timing certainly fits that theory.[288] Henry himself, in the Abbey's Foundation Charter, states somewhat broader reasons in the following manner:

> I, therefore, by the advice of my Bishops and other faithful subjects, have, for the salvation of my soul and of King William my father, of King William my brother, and of William my Son, and of Queen Matilda my mother, Queen Matilda my wife, and of all my ancestors and successors, built a new monastery at Reading...[289]

Work to clear the ground and to measure out the buildings must have taken place in early 1121 to be ready for the ceremony on 18 June that year, when the King laid the foundation stone of what was to become an astonishing and marvellous church, rivalling Westminster Abbey for both size and grandeur.[290] In January 1136 the Abbey Church became the final resting place of its founder. The 'king's tomb was situated in a place of the greatest honour, the middle of the choir to the west of the High Altar'.[291] An effigy of the King was raised over the stone tomb. The monks of the Abbey prayed for Henry's soul on the first day of every month, and over two days of special services each year on 'the anniversary of King Henry our founder'.[292]

Memorial to King Henry I Forbury Gardens

The Abbey Church has of course long since all but disappeared, with the remnants of a few associated monastic buildings to bear witness to its former glory. No tomb of King Henry exists to remind us that Reading is the resting place of one of our country's monarchs. It was this lack of a memorial to Henry I that one of the town's residents thought should be addressed.

Jamieson Boyd Hurry, by whose generosity the memorial was erected, was a well-known Reading figure. He was born in Torquay in June 1857 where his father, Rev Nicholas Hurry, had been a Congregational Minister since 1848. His first names came from the surnames of his maternal grandfather (John Boyd) and grandmother (Ann Jamieson), which came together in his mother's maiden name: Anne Shaw Jamieson Boyd.

Hurry had a peripatetic childhood as a result of his father's changes of location. The first move was to Bournemouth in the year following his birth, his father becoming the Minister of Richmond Hill St Andrews Church. From 1869 to 1871, the family lived in Neuchâtel, Switzerland, before returning to England, first to Sevenoaks (to 1873) and then Wanstead, Essex (until 1882).[293]

Hurry attended various schools, finishing his education at the City of London School, which he attended from autumn 1873 until he went up to St John's College, Cambridge, in 1876 to read Natural Sciences, and then on to St Bartholomew's Hospital, London. The list of his qualifications is impressive: BA (1880), MB and MRCS (1882), MA and MD (1885) and BC (1890).[294]

In July 1882 he took the post of ship's surgeon with the Orient & Pacific Line, first on the *Britannia*, sailing between Liverpool and Valparaiso and many ports on the way. The following year he sailed on the Steam Ship *Sorata* out to Sydney, New South Wales.[295]

He returned home to live with his parents in Wanstead before moving to Abbotsbrook, 43 Castle Street, in Reading in 1885. By 1890 he was part of May & Hurry, a partnership with the younger Mr George May (son of the surgeon, also George May, named in partnership with Isaac Harrinson in Chapter XI).[296]

By 1909 Dr Hurry had taken on a wide variety of roles in the town. From 1885 he was a member of the Reading Pathological Society, an august body founded in 1841; Honorary Secretary from 1897 to 1904 and elected President in 1908.[297]

In 1887 he was elected President of the Reading Literary and Scientific Society, a post he held for the maximum allowed two years, holding it again for the years 1904–1906. He was Honorary Secretary from 1889 until 1896, and for many years a vice president.

He was also Vice President of the Reading Natural History Society, Chairman of the Reading Branch of the St John Ambulance Association, member of the University Extension College Council and of the Reading Branch of the Parents' National Education Union, member of the Committee of Management of the Queen Victoria Institute, Reading, for the Nursing of the Poor, and Trustee of Reading Dispensary Trust. He was Deputy Chairman of the Reading Cemetery Company and a Director of the Reading Gas Company.[298]

Hurry was a prolific author of medical articles and books. When he moved from Castle Street to 'Westfield', 1 Southcote Road, in 1910, he developed an 'educational' garden with 'economic and tropical plants', which he opened to the public, usually on two or three days in July.

As a member of the Town Council's Free Library and Museum Committee he was instrumental in the provision of the library known as Battle since the late 1970s, but initially as the West End Library, then the West Reading Library. He donated the site on which the Library stands and was the Honorary Treasurer for the Voluntary Committee which campaigned to collect rate-payers' signatures and monetary gifts. Although the main capital was provided by the philanthropist Andrew Carnegie, the library would not have been built without the enthusiasm and hard work of Dr Hurry.[299]

Hurry married Gertrude, daughter of Arthur Hill of Erleigh Court, in 1892. The Arthur Hill Memorial Pool, which was built in 1911, was paid for by his children, and on land donated by his son-in-law Dr Hurry.

Hurry was also the prime mover, together with his partner George May, in the restoration of St Anne's Well in Caversham. This had been rediscovered quite by chance in January 1906 by workmen of Messrs G. W. Talbot & Son who were clearing the land.[300] The restored well was dedicated on Friday 24 April 1908 and handed over to the care of Caversham Urban District Council.[301]

However, what really brought Dr Hurry to the notice of the town was that he had become the leading expert of the time on Reading Abbey. He wrote seven books on aspects of its history, and several articles in various journals. The first book, named simply *Reading Abbey*, was published in November 1901. By 1909, the time of the proposed Memorial to Henry I, he had also written *The Rise and Fall of Reading Abbey*, published in May 1906.

At a meeting of the Town Council on Thursday 4 March 1909, the following letter was considered, addressed to the Mayor, Mr William Merrill Colebrook:

> Abbotsbrook, Reading
> February 15th, 1909
>
> To the Right Worshipful the Mayor of Reading Dear Mr Mayor,
>
> Amongst the famous events that the ancient Borough of Reading has witnessed, the founding of the Abbey on June 18th, 1121, by King Henry the First, and the burial of the same King on January 4th, 1136, hold an important place. The royal body was buried before the high altar of the splendid Abbey Church, in the presence of King Stephen and of many nobles of the realm.
>
> Such historical landmarks, which link our civic with our national life, are worthy to be kept in remembrance, since they stimulate local patriotism and a desire to promote to the utmost of our power, the beauty, prosperity and happiness of this Borough which it is our good fortune to inhabit.

In the hope of encouraging such patriotism, I have the pleasure of offering to erect in the Forbury Gardens, on the site of the Abbey Church, a memorial to its royal founder, King Henry Beauclerc. The accompanying design which has been kindly prepared by my friend, Mr W. Ravenscroft, F.S.A., indicates the form of memorial proposed, vis. an Early English cross, in silver granite, 20 feet high, with mouldings appropriate to the Plantagenet period, and an inscription recording the burial of the King in the Abbey Church at Reading.

Believe me, dear Mr Mayor,
Yours faithfully,
    Jamieson B. Hurry

The offer was readily accepted, with the Mayor commenting that 'they were greatly indebted to Dr Hurry for the years of labour he had spent in connection with the history of the Abbey' and that 'it was a most graceful act on his part, after all he had done, to give this permanent memorial to the founder'.[302]

It was decided to invite Cabinet Minister and Chief Secretary for Ireland, the Rt Hon. Augustine Birrell, to unveil the memorial cross. He had a local link, having attended Amersham Hall school in Caversham. Amersham Hall closed in 1892, the site then being taken over by Queen Anne's School, which opened in 1894.

This invitation to a prominent Cabinet Minister, however, brought some problems. He had been frequently targeted by suffragettes, and in the four months before visiting Reading, Birrell's speeches had been disrupted in Leeds, Cambridge, Bristol and Liverpool and on several occasions in London.

On two of these occasions, suffragettes had gone to some effort to disturb him. At the end of April 1909 Birrell was to speak at Colston Hall, Bristol. As had become usual, the authorities made every effort to ensure that no suffragettes were present. When Birrell rose to speak, the shout of 'Votes for women!' resounded again and again around the hall. The woman responsible was finally discovered secreted in the organ loft![303]

A week later, Birrell was at Liverpool University to receive an honorary degree when a suffragette, who had hidden herself under the stage the night before, started to shout out, 'How dare Mr Birrell face the citizens of Liverpool while a Liverpool woman is in prison for demanding a vote? You refuse to apply coercive measures to Ireland, but you apply them to British women. Shame on the Liberal Government.'[304]

As a result, Reading Council decided that they needed to take preventative action to ensure that the proceedings on 18 June were undisturbed. At least two police constables were stationed at each entrance to the Forbury Gardens to ensure only those who had been invited were allowed in. Some constables were even stationed 'behind the bushes' according to the report in the newspaper *Votes For Women*.[305]

Without any disturbance of the peace, at 4pm on Friday 18 June 1909, the memorial to Henry I was unveiled by the Rt Hon. Augustine Birrell in front of an invited audience. The memorial,

> composed of silver-grey Cornish granite, takes the form of a cross designed by architect, Mr W. Ravenscroft, F.S.A., in an architectural style appropriate to the period. The ornamentation of the head consists of early English foliage on the arms, and of the simplest form of dog-tooth ornament on the circle. Five projecting carved bosses mark the arms and the centre of the cross. The stem, with slightly sunk faces, is divided into sections by a simply rounded moulding worked into a pattern at intervals.

The massive base, composed of a single stone weighing two and a half tons, terminates above in three tiers, and rests on a broad platform of granite with steps on either side. On either side are shields of gun-metal bearing the arms of King Henry Beauclerc (gules, two lions passant guardant or) and of Reading Abbey (azure, three escallops or) respectively. The total height of the Memorial is twenty feet.

On the base is placed the following inscription:

'To the memory of Henry Beauclerc, King of England, who founded Reading Abbey on June 18th, 1121, and was buried before the High Altar on January 4th, 1136.'[306]

The fourth side of the base has an inscription noting that the memorial was the gift of Dr Hurry:

> THIS MEMORIAL,
> ERECTED BY
> DR. JAMIESON B. HURRY, M.A.,
> WAS UNVEILED
> ON JUNE 18, 1909.

About a year later, Dr Hurry proposed to make a further donation of memorials, this time 'to place in the ruins of what was formerly the Chapter-house two sculptured monuments to commemorate the life and work of the first and the last Abbot who ruled over this great monastic establishment.' These were Hugh de Boves, who became the Abbey's first abbot from 1123 to 1130, and the 31st and last abbot Hugh Cook Faringdon, abbot from 1520 until 1539. The memorials were unveiled by Sir William Osler, Regius Professor of Medicine at the University of Oxford on Monday 10 July 1911.[307] To accompany the memorial tablets, Hurry wrote a short book, *In Honour of Hugh de Boves and Hugh Cook Faringdon, First and Last Abbots of Reading*.

In December 1912, Dr Hurry proposed a further stone memorial for the Chapter House ruins in order to commemorate the writing of the 'most remarkable ancient musical composition in existence',[308] which was written down at the Abbey in the 13th century.

The commemorative tablet was unveiled by Dr H.P. Allen, of New College, Oxford, the Choragus, or Chief Choir Master, of the University. The ceremony took place on Wednesday 18 June 1913, and thus on the Abbey's 792nd anniversary. As previously, Dr Hurry produced a booklet to accompany the tablet.

The memorial tablet has a central slab of yellow magnesian limestone upon which the song is given in facsimile from the manuscript. This forms a panel in the surrounding blue Forest of Dean stone. The whole has the arms of Reading Abbey at the top and an inscription below. The tablet was designed by Mr W. Ravenscroft and produced by Mr W.S. Frith, sculptor.[309]

Between 1914 and 1926 Dr Hurry presented ten oil paintings to the town depicting historical events at the Abbey. These now adorn the Town Hall, Museum and Art Gallery.[310]

Dr Hurry made sure that the town of Reading marked the 800th anniversary of the founding of the Abbey on 18 June 1921. He wrote *The Octocentary of Reading Abbey* to coincide with the day of celebrations.

The day included a special exhibition of old manuscripts and paintings in the Art Gallery, a dramatic performance of two episodes in the life of the Abbey (the day the foundation stone was laid and the writing of *Sumer is Icumen in*) written by the Rev P.H. Ditchfield and performed in the ruins, and a concert of Old English music. Central to the day was the unveiling by the Very Rev the Dean of Winchester of a memorial tablet near the spot where King Henry Beauclerc was buried.[311] This tablet was renewed in the recent restoration of the Abbey ruins.

Not long now to the nonacentenary...

XVIII. Goldwin Smith Plaque 1910

Almost hidden in a profusion of signage, this unassuming plaque piques the passer-by's interest. Who was Professor Goldwin Smith, and why is his birthplace marked? This plaque was fixed next to the door of 15 Friar Street, Reading, in late August 1910.[312]

Shortly after Goldwin Smith died, the *Reading Observer* commented that he was 'one of the most famous men that Reading has ever produced'.[313] This is an assessment that is unlikely to be shared today, but was a well-deserved accolade.

Smith gained the reputation of a being a deep-thinking philosopher who could convey his deliberations in clear and concise prose. He was a prolific writer, producing numerous books and pamphlets, and magazine and newspaper articles. He was a journalist, biographer, poet and literary critic. He was highly regarded as a speaker, producing several series of lecture notes that sold widely and well. Not all his thoughts and beliefs gained general approval, as we shall see, but then he delighted in being thought a 'controversialist'.

As the memorial tablet states, Goldwin Smith was born on 13 August 1823 at 15 Friar Street. He later described the location thus: 'In that quiet town one of the quietest streets was Friar Street, in which my father lived.'[314]

He was the eldest of five (some sources say seven) children and the only one to live beyond 20 years of age. His father was Dr Richard Prichard Smith, a much-respected physician with a thriving practice and a reputation for benevolence to the poor. His mother, Eliza (née Breton), was of Huguenot descent. She was the niece – and almost the adopted daughter – of Thomas Goldwin, and hence her son's unusual first name.[315]

Goldwin Smith was sent to Monkton Farleigh Rectory, a private boarding school near Bath, from the age of 8. He later wrote:

> The custom of sending children to boarding-schools was, however, rather cruel. The child had not a little to suffer by severance from his home; his home affections were deadened; he was early familiarized and too often indoctrinated with evil. A boarding-school is seldom free from bullying which makes strong boys tyrants and weak boys cowards. An experienced Oxford Tutor said that his best pupils came from home with a good day-school.[316]

The experience of being away from his loved ones was not improved by the death of his mother, aged 45, in November 1833.

In 1836 he went to Eton. His fears of further bullying did not materialise, and he could write that 'bullying I neither encountered nor witnessed. Bullying was mean and Eton boys were gentlemen.' The limited classical curriculum at the time did not stretch him intellectually, and neither did every master. He wrote:

THIS HOUSE
WAS THE BIRTHPLACE OF
PROFESSOR GOLDWIN SMITH, D.C.L.
BORN AUGUST 13: 1823,
DIED AT TORONTO
JUNE 7: 1910.

'I was for two years in class under one who, though he was a good old soul and I love his memory, knew no more than I did.'[317]

While he was at Eton his father remarried. Goldwin Smith's stepmother was Katherine, daughter of Sir Nathaniel Dukinfield. Although he wrote very positively of her ('She was an excellent woman, managed her household admirably, and was very good to the poor, who thronged her funeral when she died'),[318] they were never at ease together. One relative thought this was because the stepmother was in awe of her stepson's intellect and feared speaking any opinion in his presence.[319]

In May 1841 Goldwin Smith matriculated at Christ Church College, Oxford, and a year later transferred to Magdalen with a 'Demyship' (scholarship).[320] He had been nominated for the Demyship by Magdalen's President, Martin Routh. In addition to his role at Oxford, Routh was Rector of Tilehurst, and had married Eliza Blagrave, daughter of John Blagrave of Calcot Park, in 1820.

Goldwin Smith graduated in the First Class in Classics at Oxford in 1845, having won the Hertford and Ireland Scholarships (for Latin and Greek respectively) and the Chancellor's prizes for Latin verse and for an English essay along the way. He was subsequently elected to the Stowell Fellowship in Civil Law at University College.[321]

He had become a student at Lincoln's Inn in November 1842 (at age 19, while also studying at Oxford) and spent much of his time in London after he graduated. Although he enjoyed studying law, especially as he felt that it honed his reasoning skills, he decided that the profession was not for him. He was called to the Bar on 11 June 1850,[322] but never practised. In 1848, while he was living in London, his father retired from his medical practice and moved from Friar Street to the country, residing in Mortimer House.

The 1850s were a busy time for Goldwin Smith. In his *Reminiscences* he wrote:

> My life during the years that followed was rather a medley. I was for a time Tutor at University College; was Assistant Secretary to the Royal Commission of Inquiry into the University of Oxford; and Secretary to the Parliamentary Commission of Reform which followed it; tried the study of law for a time in London, but found that the profession would be beyond my strength; fell back on the University; and became Regius Professor of Modern History; during my tenure of which office I was a member of the National Education Commission.[323]

These were the years when he made a national name for himself, especially through his role in University reform. He was a very popular Regius Professor of Modern History, drawing large crowds of students to his lectures – including

Plaque at 15 Friar Street

the Prince of Wales, later King Edward VII. Smith was Regius Professor from 1858 to 1866, at which time he resigned. There were many who expressed surprise – shock even – that anyone could give up such an august post. The official reason given was for Goldwin Smith to concentrate on his writing. The real reason, however, was that he returned to Mortimer to look after his father, who was gradually descending into insanity.[324]

Dr Smith's mental health continued to deteriorate. After suffering for nearly two years he took his own life by drinking prussic acid in October 1867.[325] There is a brass plaque remembering the Smith family in St Laurence's Church, on the north wall underneath one of the windows. The family tomb in the churchyard is just the other side of the wall, although it is now difficult to read. It is the first tomb on the right-hand side of the footpath leading from Market Place to the churchyard. All the family, except Goldwin Smith, are buried there.

The first rumour of Goldwin Smith emigrating to the United States appeared in the newspapers the following month.[326] In *Some Worthies of Reading*, J.J. Cooper wrote: 'Dr Prichard Smith came to a tragic end... and Goldwin's suffering in mind and body was serious, and in the hope of recovering health and tone by change of scene he had thought of returning to America, which he had already visited in 1864.'[327] Cornell University had been founded in 1865 in Ithaca, New York State, and was seeking to attract professors. In 1868 Goldwin Smith met Andrew White, President of the University, and accepted his proposal to become an honorary professor of English and Constitutional History, on the condition that he would be unpaid and that 'his time would be at his own disposal.'[328]

After just three years Goldwin Smith left his post at Cornell, becoming a non-resident professor and moving to Toronto. In his *Reminiscences* he gave as his reason for the move that he 'yearned for a rather more domestic life' and that Toronto had the advantage of being where a branch of his family lived.[329]

In 1875 Goldwin Smith married Harriet Elizabeth Mann Boulton, who had been widowed eighteen months previously. They lived happily together for 34 years at the Grange, a 'charming house in its own grounds situated at the very centre of Toronto',[330] thus finally giving him the domestic life he craved.

Goldwin Smith was best known for his journalism, and to a lesser extent for books on politics and history. His books included: *Irish History and Irish Character* (1861); *The Empire* (1863), which garnered much criticism by suggesting that Gibraltar should be abandoned and the colonies should be self-governing; *Three English Statesmen* (1867) on Pym, Cromwell and Pitt; *The United States: An Outline of Political History 1492–1871* (1893), which was described as a literary masterpiece; and *The United Kingdom: A Political History* (1899). He elicited strong reactions in his adopted land to many of his writings, not least his 1891 book, *Canada and the Canadian Question*, in which he opined that Canada should become part of the United States.

He wrote frequently for a range of newspapers and journals, beginning with the *Morning Chronicle* in the 1850s, *Daily News* from the early 1860s, and

Macmillan's Magazine from May 1864. His second article in that magazine, in February 1865, was entitled 'President Lincoln', and was based on a personal interview Goldwin Smith had had with the recently re-elected President.[331]

When in Toronto, he edited *Canadian Monthly* (1872–4) and founded *Nation* (1874), *Bystander* (1880) and *Week*, which became the principal literary and political journal in Canada, in 1884.[332] Goldwin Smith also wrote two literary biographies: *Cowper* (1880) and *Jane Austen* (1887), the latter being one of the first critical analyses of Austen's works.

In June 1882 Oxford University conferred on him an honorary DCL (Doctor of Civil Law). The citation speech by an Oxford Professor was in Latin, but thankfully the newspaper report had a translation:

> In presenting Mr Goldwin Smith, the learned professor descanted on his early distinctions at Oxford, his eminence as a writer, and the gravity of his thoughts, and the trenchant power of his style. He alluded in glowing terms to Mr Smith's ardent patriotism, and his achievements as a political controversialist, and said that although he had settled in Canada, Oxford still claimed him, and he could not escape either the affection of his friends or the honours of his university.[333]

Harriet died at the Grange on 9 September 1909, aged 82. In early February 1910, Goldwin Smith slipped on some ice and broke his thigh. He never recovered from the accident, although in April he was able to be carried down to his library, so that he could resume his correspondence and writing. He grew steadily weaker and died in his library on 7 June, aged 86.[334] He was buried in St James' Cemetery in Toronto.

Goldwin Smith's death was reported throughout Britain. The *Reading Observer* wrote:

> Reading has been the birthplace of not a few famous men, the names of whom will readily occur to our readers. Very prominent among these has always been Professor Goldwin Smith, who has just died at his home in Toronto at the mature age of 88 (sic), having been born on the 13th August 1823. He was a great historian and a prolific writer, and there were very few of the pinnacles of fame as a great scholar that he did not climb...[335]

In Canada, J.W. Longley wrote of Smith that everything he wrote was 'read and quoted throughout all the English-speaking world, and at his death he received the universal homage of the intellectual world'.[336]

In August 1910, plans were in place in Reading for a memorial:

> With the consent, kindly accorded, of Mr J.H. Walters, the owner of the large red-brick house, No. 15, Friar-street, Reading, a recording tablet, noting it as the birthplace of the late Professor Goldwin Smith, is shortly to be inserted in the front of the house. The Mayor of Reading [Mr William

Frame] has interested himself in the matter and warmly endorsed the suggestion. Those of our readers who know and appreciate the writing of the great Professor of History will rejoice that his memory should be kept in evidence in a permanent way in the town of his birth.[337]

On Cornell University's Central Campus, in front of Goldwin Smith Hall, is a stone bench upon which is carved: *Above all nations is humanity*, a phrase Goldwin Smith is said to have coined. He donated this bench and arranged for the inscription in 1871. By the terms of his will, he left almost his entire estate, amounting to about $750,000, as an endowment to Cornell University.

On 1 February 1912 Dr Jamieson B. Hurry presented a portrait of Goldwin Smith to Reading Corporation. The portrait, showing the professor seated in his favourite armchair, was painted by Canadian artist John Russell. At the same time, the Corporation funded the printing of copies of *Goldwin Smith D.C.L.: A Brief Account of His Life and Writings* by J.J. Cooper.

The Chairman of the Reading Public Libraries Committee, Mr F. A. Cox, wrote to the *Reading Observer* on the presentation of the painting to remind readers that 'our Public Library contains the undermentioned works by our late great literary townsman',[338] with a list of 12 volumes. The current listing is much longer: 34 items in the Reference Stock, and one copy of Goldwin Smith's *Reminiscences* on the shelves.

XIX. War Memorial 1932

The Reading and Berkshire War Memorial was unveiled on Wednesday 27 July 1932 in memory of almost ten thousand Berkshire men who had died in the First World War.

Most memorials to the fallen of the Great War were erected by the early 1920s. The Cenotaph in Brock Barracks, Oxford Road, in memory of the officers and men of the Royal Berkshire Regiment, was unveiled in September 1921, for example.[339]

There had been discussions about a County memorial since 1919 but progress was not exactly swift. In April 1921, the *Reading Observer* commented sarcastically, in the context of Berkshire historical landmarks, that:

> Not perhaps in two generations, but a few decades (let us trust) hence, there will be a Berkshire war memorial, and that will be another interesting milestone for the inhabitants of Berkshire to look upon circa A.D. 2000. Even if it is not erected, the designs will probably be on view by then.[340]

In fact, by this date the Executive Committee of the Berkshire War Memorial had decided upon a design called 'Winged Victory' by Professor J. Harvard Thomas of London University and Mr Mervyn L. Macartney, ARIBA.[341] The estimated cost was £8,000 and a public appeal was launched. However, by February 1922 just £1,000 had been subscribed.[342]

By the end of the year the memorial project had been dropped in favour of a scheme to provide a headquarters in Reading for the Red Cross Society. This did not materialise either.[343]

In November 1922 the outgoing Mayor, Councillor W. R. Howell, said that, while 'he had commenced with high hopes that a decided step forward in connection with the Berkshire and Reading War Memorial would have been made during his mayorality', he regretted that nothing definite had been achieved.[344]

Nothing more was done until Councillor F. G. Sainsbury became Mayor some years later. In April 1931 he called a meeting of the former committee and those who had subscribed to the fund. It was agreed at that meeting to disband the old committee and create a new one, calling together 'representative men and women ... for the purpose of formulating and carrying out a scheme for the erection in Reading of a memorial in honour of the men of Reading and Berkshire who lost their lives in the Great War.'[345]

By the end of 1922 £1,100 had been collected. From that sum, the architects' fees and other costs had had to be paid, so just £653 6s. 7d. remained in 1931 for the new committee.

Berkshire Society of Architects generously offered to arrange a competition to find the best locally produced design. T. Lawrence Dale, FRIBA, a well-known architect (and at this time the Oxford Diocesan Surveyor) agreed to be the assessor and chose the best three designs from those submitted for the War

111

Memorial Committee to choose from. The winning design was by E. Leslie Gunston, ARIBA, from Emmer Green, whose design was:

> a monument of a graceful shaft on steps with incised crosses at the top and an ingenious method of flood lighting introduced into the steps. The committee were largely influenced by the desirability of not blocking the entrance or view of the gardens.[346]

Tenders were invited to produce the memorial, and by early June Collier & Catley Ltd of St Mary's Butts had been employed. Work proceeded apace and in a few short weeks the memorial was erected and ready for its unveiling ceremony.[347]

The date chosen was 27 July, the anniversary of the Battle of Maiwand where many Berkshire men had lost their lives in 1880, and whose memorial was of course a short distance away in the Forbury. Many thousands were expected to attend the ceremony. Ten thousand copies of the order of proceedings were printed and distributed on the day. So that all could properly take part, a microphone and five loudspeakers were installed.

The Service of Dedication began at 3.30pm with the singing of the hymn 'O Valiant Hearts', led by the boys of Blue Coat School and accompanied by the Band of the 4th Battalion Royal Berks Regiment. After the Lord's Prayer and readings from the Bible, the Chairman of the Memorial Committee, Councillor F.G. Sainsbury, invited the Lord Lieutenant of Berkshire, Mr James Herbert Benyon, to unveil the memorial. Prior to removing the Union Jack that covered the memorial, the Lord Lieutenant said:

> Nearly fourteen years ago the Great War ended and we, people of Berkshire, are assembled here today with one purpose only – to honour our dead. Nearly ten thousand of our men lost their lives in the struggle between nations, and at last we have within our midst a memorial which will help us always to remember that they did their duty and died. This is a day of remembrance – we can forget the delays which have occurred, and which have prevented until now the erection of a memorial for the county and county town as a whole. A few months ago, the delays loomed large in our minds and we were grieved, but now they can be forgotten, for a memorial exists and we can begin again to remember that brave men lost their lives and that we are here today as citizens of a free country. There are in this country many war memorials, and it is right that there should be. It is also right that there should be a memorial for this county as a whole, and today we join together – men and women in all walks of life and of all creeds – to do honour to Berkshire men who died during four years of awful war. Those who were in Reading in the autumn months of

War Memorial outside the Victoria Gate to the Forbury

1914 will never forget how the men of the town and the country flocked to the barracks of the Royal Berkshire Regiment to enlist, and how they were to be seen in the streets of the town during their early training. Many men joined other units and other branches of the nation's forces, and we can remember with pride that they did not fail their country in time of need. The Maiwand Memorial a few yards away reminds us that Berkshire men were not afraid 52 years ago today; this memorial that I am about to unveil reminds us that our own men, our kith and kin, faced the ordeal of war steadfastly and bravely. It reminds us, too, that we owe them a debt that we can never repay, and it behoves us never to forget their sacrifice of the greatest treasure they possessed – life. This memorial is a simple one, but so long as it stands it will help the living to honour the dead, and I am proud that the task of unveiling it has fallen on me. On behalf of all the inhabitants of Berkshire, including the county town of Reading, I unveil this memorial to the honour of brave men.

The memorial was then unveiled. The Last Post was sounded, followed by one minute's silence. The Mayor's Chaplain, Rev H. A. Bullock, Vicar of St Laurence, then solemnly dedicated the memorial with words by Robert Laurence Binyon:

> With proud thanksgiving let us remember our Elder Brethren:
> They shall grow not old, as we that are left grow old
> Age shall not weary them, nor the years condemn.
> At the going down of the sun and in the morning
> We will remember them.

The assembled throng then sang 'O God, our help in ages past', after which wreaths were placed on the memorial steps. The Reveille then sounded, followed by a blessing by the Mayor's Chaplain and the singing of the National Anthem.

The final part of the ceremony was less formal. Anyone who so wished was allowed to come forward and lay a floral tribute by the memorial.[348]

The words on the front of the memorial have since been altered to include the dates of the Second World War and an additional letter 's' at the very end:

> The Glorious Dead 1914–1918
> 1939 –1945
>
> To the honoured memory of the
> men of Reading and Berkshire
> who gave their lives for King and
> Country during the Great Wars

Just in front of the War Memorial, a commemorative paving slab was unveiled at a ceremony on 21 August 2015 by Anne Ames in honour of her grandfather, Trooper Fred Potts vc. Exactly one hundred years before, Potts was injured in a

Berkshire Yeomanry Brigade assault on Scimitar Hill, Gallipoli. What happened next earned him the Victoria Cross. The citation stated:

> For most conspicuous bravery and devotion to a wounded comrade in the Gallipoli Peninsula.
>
> Although himself severely wounded in the thigh in the attack on 'Hill 70' on 21st August, 1915, he remained out over 48 hours under the Turkish trenches with a private of his Regiment who was severely wounded and unable to move, although he could himself have returned to safety.
>
> Finally he fixed a shovel to the equipment of his wounded comrade, and, using this as a sledge, he dragged him back over 600 yards to our lines, though fired at by the Turks on the way. He reached our trenches at about 9.30pm on August 23rd.[349]

Trooper Frederick William Owen Potts was aged 22 at the time, and before mobilisation lived with his parents at 54 Edgehill Street, Reading. He worked at the Pulsometer Engineering Works and was a member of the St Giles Branch of the Church of England's Men's Society.

He received his medal from King George V at a ceremony in Buckingham Palace on 9 December 1915. By then he had become Lance-Corporal Potts, and within a week he was a married man. He married Ruth Wellstead, eldest daughter of Mr & Mrs J.T. Wellstead of Rowley Road, Reading, at St Giles' Church on Wednesday 15 December.[350]

A short distance along The Forbury, near the Abbey Gateway, stands the main memorial to Trooper Potts, a striking life-sized statue of Potts dragging his comrade, Trooper Arthur Andrews, to safety. It was designed and sculpted by Tom Murphy of Liverpool. The statue was unveiled on 4 October 2015 by the Lord-Lieutenant of the Royal County of Berkshire, Mr James Puxley, and television personality Mr Chris Tarrant OBE. Nearby, the Roll of Honour of the Berkshire Yeomanry, with the names of 426 men who had died as a result of their service, was unveiled by two students from The Abbey School, Lois Gaskell and Emma Shepherd.

The funding for the combined memorials was achieved through huge effort by the Trooper Potts VC Memorial Trust, which raised almost £200,000.

There are two other war memorials nearby, both in the Forbury Gardens. Next to the bandstand is a plaque marking the 50th anniversary of the D-Day landings in June 1944, 'commemorating those Reading people who gave their lives for our freedom'. The memorial was unveiled by the Deputy Mayor, Cllr John Oliver, on 6 June 1994.

In a grove among the roses near Forbury Hill, there is a memorial stone for the Reading & District Burma Star Association, remembering the sacrifice of those local men who fought in the Far East against the Japanese in 1941 to 1945. This simple memorial stone replaced a similar pre-existing stone in 2010, funded with the help of local funeral directors A.B. Walker & Son.[351]

XX. Spanish Civil War Memorial 1990

The Memorial to those from or with strong connections to Reading who died in the Spanish Civil War (1936–1939) now stands in Forbury Gardens. It was originally placed near the Civic Offices (now demolished) and was first unveiled on 5 May 1990.

The Spanish Civil War was, broadly, a conflict between the left-wing Republican government and the Nationalists, supported by Fascist Italy and Nazi Germany. The Republicans received support from Communist Soviet Union, and from many volunteers from Europe and the USA who were organised into International Brigades.

It is thought that almost 20 people with connections to Reading volunteered either to fight or to serve in relief or support services in an International Brigade.[352] There is uncertainty over some records and work to research them continues. The memorial in the Forbury names three Reading men killed in the war, but one of them – George Middleton – is now thought to have been an invention. Further research has also brought to light Anthony Carrit and Julian Bell, ambulance drivers, killed during the battle of Brunete in July 1937.

In July 1986 there was a well-attended meeting in the Reading Civic Centre to commemorate the 50th anniversary of the outbreak of the war. Prior discussion about producing a memorial in Reading culminated at this meeting with the decision to form a committee, to be chaired by Ray Parkes, to decide on the form of the memorial and to raise funds for it. Present at this meeting were three of those who went to join the International Brigades in Spain: Thora Craig (née Silverthorne), a nurse; Reg Saxton, a doctor; and Jimmy Moon, a soldier.[353]

The committee commissioned local sculptor Eric Stanford to produce the memorial. Eric Stanford was Keeper of Art at Reading Museum and was given paid leave of absence by Reading Borough Council to undertake the task. The University of Reading generously provided a studio for the sculptor to work in.

On Saturday 5 May 1990 the memorial, wrapped in the Spanish Republic's flag, was unveiled. The *Evening Post* reported:

> Reading has paid tribute to the volunteers who fought in the Spanish Civil War against the forces of fascism. A stone statue in memory of the 10 Reading men and women who went to Spain during the 1936–1939 war was unveiled by Reading mayor Maureen Lockey on Saturday…
>
> Coun. Lockey said: 'It is a great pleasure to unveil this statue. It is a memorial to what these people did for Reading and for Spain.'

Memorial statue remembering Reading volunteers killed fighting in the Spanish Civil War

Ray Parkes, chairman of the Reading International Brigade memorial committee said the conflict should have been called the Spanish Anti-Fascist War. Actor Tom Radcliffe then gave a reading from the Requiem Mass by Jack Lindsey.[354]

The statue, in Portland stone, depicts, on its front, a mother with a dead child in her arms, symbolising Spain mourning over the death of the young Spanish Republic.[355] Beneath the mother's feet is the legend

1936 SPAIN 1939

On the sides of the statue is written 'Volunteers for Peace' and 'Defended Democracy'. The reverse of the statue is not now easy to see, but shows three soldiers, armed with guns. Below, on the base, are the names of those from Reading who were known or believed to have died during the Civil War when the statue was carved:

DIED FOR LIBERTY
GEORGE MIDDLETON CASA DE GAMPO
– NOVEMBER 1936 –
WILLIAM BALL JARAMA
– FEBRUARY 1937 –
ARCHIBALD FRANCIS ARAGON
– MARCH 1938 –

With the demolition of the Civic Offices in early 2015, a new home was needed for the statue. It was also in great need of cleaning and restoration after almost 25 years. The latter entailed more fundraising by the Reading International Brigade Memorial Committee.

On Sunday 10 May 2015 the statue, now in Forbury Gardens next to Abbots Walk, was unveiled at a ceremony at noon led by Reading Mayor Tony Jones.

Cllr Jones said: 'I am very pleased to see this memorial – and an important part of Reading's heritage – renovated and relocated to the Abbey Quarter. The re-dedication service will honour and remember those Reading residents who fought for freedom and democracy in the Spanish Civil War.'

Ray Parkes, an author who chronicled the town's involvement, said: 'After 25 years it's wonderful to see this nationally regarded monument returned to its original condition, and relocated to such an historic setting. We'd like to express our profound thanks to the mayor, Reading Borough Council, and all the many individuals and organisations who so generously gave money and time to make this possible.'[356]

The Reading International Brigades Memorial Trust published a leaflet, 'Defended Democracy', to accompany the relocation and rededication of the statue.[357] In the leaflet the authors listed those believed to have been from Reading or with significant connection to Reading who served in Spain.

Ray Parkes, the Reading International Brigade Memorial Committee Chairman, wrote of the statue that 'it is there not just to remind us of the commitment and courage of our heroes who fought and died fighting fascism, but that freedom everywhere was never achieved without struggle and sacrifice.'[358]

Endnotes and sources

1. Crawfurd pages 4 and 34
2. Coates page 230, which quotes the Register of St Laurence's Church that they were married on 23 September 1616
3. Berkshire Record Office reference D/QR 32/3 Conveyance Deed of Sir Thomas Vachel's charity
4. Berkshire Record Office reference D/QR 32/1 Trust Deed of Sir Thomas Vachel's charity. Also see Coates page 135; Man 1816 page 408; Doran pages 250–251
5. *Berkshire Chronicle* 3 February 1866 page 1 column 2
6. Coates pages 133–134; Man 1816 pages 395–396; Doran page 249
7. Man 1816 page 402; Doran page 249
8. Blandy page 15
9. Coates page 134; Man 1816 page 407; Doran page 250
10. Coates page 135; Man 1816 pages 412–413; Doran pages 251–252
11. *Berkshire Chronicle* 20 July 1861 page 5 column 4
12. Berkshire Record Office reference D/QR 2/1/1 *Minutes of the Trustees of the Church Charities of the Borough of Reading 1837 to 1866*, meetings of 13 and 24 July 1863
13. *Berkshire Chronicle* 19 March 1864 page 3 column 2
14. Ibid. 10 September 1864 page 4 column 1
15. Berkshire Record Office reference D/QR 2/1/1 *Minutes of the Trustees of the Church Charities of the Borough of Reading 1837 to 1866*, meetings of 21 March 1866 and 11 May 1866. Also see *Berkshire Chronicle* 17 February 1866 page 5 column 3
16. *Reading Mercury* 22 April 1865 page 6 column 1
17. Ibid. and see *Berkshire Chronicle* 22 April 1865 page 6 columns 1 to 3
18. *Reading Mercury* 24 March 1866 page 6 column 7
19. Blandy page 30
20. Charity number 1152759
21. *Reading Mercury* 24 July 1954 page 3 column 3; also *Reading Standard* 23 July 1954 page 3 column 4. The incident is also described in North page 66
22. historicengland.org.uk [Accessed October 2017]. List Entry Number 1154678
23. readingalmshouses.org.uk [Accessed October 2017]
24. Hurry 1917 page 110
25. Hurry 1901 page 24
26. Quoted in Coates page 268
27. Ibid. page 64
28. Guilding (Ed.) 1896 page 323
29. Kerry pages 18 and 20; see also Coates page 188 and *Reading Mercury* 25 January 1868 page 5 column 2

30 Guilding (Ed.) 1896 pages 48, 125, 258, 332, 410
31 *Reading Mercury* 22 March 1862 page 5 column 3
32 Field page 10
33 Either Mr Richard Simeon or his son John, at this date Recorder of Reading
34 Berkshire Record Office reference R/AC1/1/24 *Diary of the Corporation 1786–1809*, entry for 18 August 1796
35 Ibid. 18 September 1799
36 Sowan 2007 is a very good re-telling of the Obelisk's story
37 Carus page 2
38 *Windsor and Eton Express* 13 December 1812 page 4 column 4
39 Man 1816 page 213
40 Ibid. page 420
41 Berkshire Record Office reference R/AC1/1/24 *Diary of the Corporation of Reading 1786–1809*
42 Ibid. Meeting of 31 January 1804
43 J. J. Cooper page 54
44 Summers pages 53 and 54
45 Windsor page 277
46 collections.soane.org/object-mr39 [Accessed September 2017]
47 Berkshire Record Office reference R/AC1/1/24 *Diary of the Corporation of Reading 1786–1809* meeting of 15 May 1804
48 Gunnis page 364. Quoted in Sowan 2007 page 8
49 Windsor page 278
50 *Reading Mercury* 10 September 1804 page 3 columns 2 to 3
51 Ibid. 17 September 1804 page 1 column 2
52 Ibid. page 3 columns 2 and 3
53 Ibid. 24 September 1804 page 3 columns 2 to 4
54 Ibid. 8 October 1804 page 3 columns 1 to 3. The final couplet is a quotation from Richard Tickell's 1778 satirical poem 'The Wreath of Fashion, or, The Art of Sentimental Poetry'
55 These can be clearly seen in an 1807 drawing in the *Reading Chronicle* 16 August 2007 page 13
56 Berkshire Record Office reference R/AC1/1/24 *Diary of the Corporation of Reading 1786–1809* meeting of 11 January 1805
57 Ibid. Also see *Reading Mercury* 6 May 1805 page 3 column 2
58 Blandy page 41
59 Man 1810 pages 40 to 43
60 The water pump is not on W. H. Timms' 1823 drawing of the Market Place (see, for example Hylton 1994 image 7), but can be clearly seen on George Sidney Shepherd's sketch of 1832 (*Reading Chronicle* 16 August 2007 page 13)
61 historicengland.org.uk [Accessed September 2018]. The Simeon Monument is List Entry Number 1113534
62 Sowan 2007 pages 16 to 18 gives a good overview of these changes
63 *Reading Chronicle* 16 August 2007 page 13

64 Information about Braag's early life is taken from Ryberg page 66, Svend E. Holsoe *Virgin Island Families*: Braag (2011) online at ancestry.co.uk [Accessed March 2018] and the Danish Demographic Database at ddd.dda.dk/ddd_en [Accessed March 2018] for the 1787 census. With thanks to John Nixon for discussion of the family details.
65 *Reading Mercury* 13 October 1800 and 2 June 1806, both cited in Childs page 58
66 *Reading Mercury* 16 November 1807 page 3 column 3. Also see Nixon page 4 and Table 1 on page 14
67 *The General Entry Book of Danish Prisoners of War at Reading* held at the National Archives, Kew
68 Ibid.
69 Ditchfield (Ed.) 1887 page 34
70 *Reading Mercury* 21 December 1807 page 3 column 4
71 hansard.millbanksystems.com [Accessed March 2018]
72 Details from *The General Entry Book of Danish Prisoners of War at Reading, op. cit.*, and Nixon Table 3 page 15
73 Berkshire Record Office reference D/P98 Burials 1653–1902
74 *Reading Mercury* 12 September 1808 page 3 column 2
75 Ibid. 3 October 1808 page 3 column 2, 10 October 1808 page 3 column 2, 17 October 1808 page 3 column 2
76 See Nixon Table 2 on page 14 and Table 4 on page 15
77 *Reading Mercury* 30 October 1809 page 3 column 2. For the model ship, see collections.readingmuseum.org.uk [Accessed March 2018]
78 Nixon page 11. Also see Table 1 page 14
79 Ditchfield (Ed.) 1887 page 7
80 Darter page 66
81 Ibid. page 19. Also see Childs page 58
82 Ditchfield (Ed.) 1887 page 22
83 Nixon page 5, referring to endnote 12 on page 12. Hinton page 146, while not using the title *Gentlemen Danes*, has a good summary of their time in Reading
84 Berkshire Record Office St Laurence's Parish Records. Also see *The General Entry Book of Danish Prisoners of War at Reading, op. cit.* There were other marriages too. On 7 December 1813 there was a double wedding at St Laurence's, with two Danes marrying two sisters: Lourens Ludying married Sarah Kingston and Frederick W. de Frederici married Elizabeth Kingston. On 7 February 1814 Peter Hemsen, formerly Mate of the Merchant Vessel Wilhemina, married Harriett Mellett, also in St Laurence's.
85 Hylton 1994 image 11
86 getreading.co.uk article by Linda Fort 30 October 2009 'Ceremony remembers a "Gentleman Dane"'. Also see readingchronicle.co.uk article 6 November 2009 'From Reading to the people of Denmark'. [Both accessed March 2018]

87 Childs pages 27–28 has a good description of the fairs at the end of the 18th and beginning of the 19th century.
88 Man 1816 *op. cit.* pages 135–136
89 John Spicer, Reading born and a former pupil of Reading School, was Head Master 1750–1771. See Naxton page 89
90 *Reading Mercury* 10 June 1776 page 2 column 2
91 Ibid. 17 June 1776 page 3 column 1
92 See roundmoundsproject.wordpress.com [Accessed August 2018]
93 *Reading Mercury* 25 July 1774 page 1 column 3
94 Ibid. 1 July 1799 page 3 column 2
95 *Forbury Hill: A Poem* (Rivington, London 1813). The poem is dated at Reading, September 1812
96 Ditchfield (Ed.) 1887 *op. cit.* entry for 20 May 1816
97 Ibid. 20, 25 and 27 February 1817
98 *Reading Mercury* 11 January 1790 page 2 column 3
99 Ibid. 28 March 1796 page 3 column 3
100 Ibid. 22 March 1830 page 3 column 2. She was buried at St Laurence's Church on 23 March 1830 (Parish Record)
101 Ibid. 29 November 1830 page 3 column 1
102 *Berkshire Chronicle* 12 February 1831 page 4 column 2
103 *Reading Mercury* 9 May 1831 page 3 columns 1 and 2
104 Ibid. 24 October 1831 page 3 column 3; *Berkshire Chronicle* 2 October 1831 page 4 column 5. Harriet died on 11 July 1836 – see *Reading Mercury* 18 July 1836 page 3 column 3. She was buried on 15 July 1836 at St Laurence's (Parish record).
105 *Reading Mercury* 8 April 1833 page 3 column 3
106 Ibid. 22 April 1833 page 3 column 3. This incident is referred to in Slade page 88, although not with its sequel.
107 *Reading Mercury* 8 May 1852 page 3 column 4
108 Joshua Vines died aged 85 on 3 October 1846 – see *Reading Mercury* 10 October 1846 page 3 column 4. He was buried at St Laurence's six days later (Parish record).
109 *Reading Mercury* 21 March 1840 page 3 column 3
110 *Berkshire Chronicle* 21 March 1840 page 3 column 1
111 Ibid. 14 March 1840 page 3 column 5. The Morning Post 1 April 1840 page 4 column 6 adds the detail that the Directors can non-stop from Paddington and took 45 minutes to reach Reading.
112 *Reading Mercury* 28 March 1840 page 3 column 3, and *Berkshire Chronicle* 28 March 1840 page 5 column 2
113 *Reading Mercury* 4 April 1840 page 3 column 3
114 National Railway Museum website citation: 'Science Museum Group. In memory of Henry West. 2001-8638' Science Museum Group Collection Online collection.sciencemuseum.org.uk [Accessed October 2017]
115 Bronze plaque – see blueplaqueplaces.co.uk [Accessed October 2017]
116 *Berkshire Chronicle* 4 April 1840 page 3 column 2. See also Sowan 2013 page 13–14

117 *Reading Mercury* 28 July 1860 page 5 columns 4 and 5. *Berkshire Chronicle* 28 July 1860 page 5 column 2
118 Charles P. Melly, 'A Paper on Drinking Fountains', 1858, liverpoolmonuments.co.uk [Accessed September 2017]
119 *Morning Chronicle* 23 April 1859 page 3 column 6
120 *Berkshire Chronicle* 2 July 1859 page 5 column 1
121 In the *Reading Mercury* 23 July 1859 page 5 column 2 there is a mention in passing in a report of the third Summer Festival of the Reading Juvenile Temperance Society, or Band of Hope, of three cheers for Mr W. Palmer, as Treasurer, and for 'the public drinking fountain erected at his expense in the Forbury'. However, it is not until two years later (see for example *Reading Mercury* 24 August 1861 page 2 column 4) that William Palmer actually presents a drinking fountain in the Forbury to the Council.
122 *Berkshire Chronicle* 12 November 1859 page 3 column 2
123 Ibid. 27 May 1865 page 5 column 1
124 Ibid. 3 June 1865 page 4 column 4
125 *Reading Mercury* 28 July 1860 page 5 columns 4 to 5
126 Ibid. 11 August 1860 page 5 column 3
127 historicengland.org.uk [Accessed April 2018]. Grade II Listed, List Entry Number 1156250
128 Stacpoole-Ryding page 44. The Regiment arrived at Kandahar on 25 March 1880.
129 Ibid. page 51
130 Ibid. Chapter IV, pages 53–72
131 Ibid. page 104
132 *Berkshire Chronicle* 31 July 1880 page 2 columns 2 and 3; *Reading Mercury* 31 July 1880 page 2 column 2
133 *Reading Mercury* 14 August 1880 page 5 columns 3 and 4
134 Ibid. 30 October 1880 page 6 column 2
135 Ibid. 29 July 1882 page 5 column 2
136 Ibid. 13 November 1880 page 6 column 2
137 Ibid. 19 February 1881 page 6 column 2; also see *Berkshire Chronicle* page 5 column 5
138 *Berkshire Chronicle* 3 September 1881 page 4 column 2; also see *Reading Chronicle* page 4 column 7
139 *Reading Mercury* 7 January 1882 page 5 column 4 and 30 January 1886 page 2 column 1
140 *Reading Mercury* 21 June 1884 page 5 column 2
141 Ibid. 11 October 1884 page 5 column 2
142 Ibid. 30 January 1886 page 2 column 1
143 Ibid. 13 November 1886 page 5 column 3
144 Ibid. 24 December 1886 page 2 columns 1 to 3; also see *Berkshire Chronicle* 24 December 1886 page 2 columns 2 to 5
145 *Berkshire Chronicle* 20 November 1909 page 1 column 5
146 See Simonds Family website at simondsfamily.me.uk [Accessed October 2017]
147 *Reading Mercury* 5 February 1887 page 5 column 6
148 Ibid. page 6 column 6

149 *Berkshire Chronicle* 19 February 1887 page 2 column 3
150 *Reading Mercury* 12 March 1887 page 2 column 5
151 Ibid. 7 May 1887 page 5 column 3
152 *Berkshire Chronicle* 25 June 1887 page 2 column 1
153 Ibid. column 2
154 Ibid. 6 August 1887 page 8 column 3, reporting on the Town Council meeting of 4 August.
155 Ibid. 4 July 1903 page 10 column 4
156 historicengland.org.uk [Accessed August 2017] List Entry Number 1113571
157 *Berkshire Chronicle* 4 December 1886 page 5 column 5
158 *Reading Mercury* 2 April 1887 page 5 column 2
159 *Berkshire Chronicle* 30 July 1887 page 2 column 2
160 Ibid. 5 March 1887 page 6 column 1
161 *Reading Mercury* 7 May 1887 page 5 column 3
162 *Berkshire Chronicle* 25 June 1887 page 8 column 6
163 *Reading Mercury* 23 July 1887 page 5 column 2
164 *Berkshire Chronicle* 23 July 1887 page 5 column 4
165 Ibid. 6 August 1887 page 8 column 3
166 *Reading Mercury* 30 July 1887 page 2 columns 1 to 3
167 Ibid. 6 August 1887 page 5 column 2
168 For the full Statement of Income and Expenditure of the Reading Jubilee Fund, see *Berkshire Chronicle* 12 November 1887 page 4 column 3
169 *Berkshire Chronicle* 5 November 1887 page 2 column 4
170 See the 16 January 2014 getreading article by Brendan Carr, on getreading.co.uk [Accessed August 2017]
171 historicengland.org.uk [Accessed August 2017] List Entry Number 1113483
172 George May wrote as a testimonial to Isaac Harrinson, when the latter was seeking to be appointed as Resident Medical Officer at the Royal Berkshire Hospital, that Isaac Harrinson had resided with him nearly four years, dated 2 February 1839 – see *Berkshire Chronicle* 16 February 1839 page 1 column 2. Hurry 1909 page 87 states that he had come to Reading in 1839, but this is therefore incorrect.
173 National Probate Calendar for 1888. Harrinson's estate was in excess of £45,000.
174 *Reading Mercury* 13 April 1844 page 3 column 5
175 *Berkshire Burials*, Berkshire Family History Society
176 *Reading Mercury* 7 July 1888 page 2 column 4
177 *Reading Mercury* 9 September 1865 page 5 column 2. See also Harrinson's statement in *Reading Mercury* 24 December 1887 page 2 column 5
178 *Berkshire Chronicle* 18 June 1864 page 5 column 3; 30 September 1876 page 5 column 4
179 Ibid. 19 October 1872 page 5 column 3
180 Ibid. 20 May 1865 page 6 column 1
181 *Reading Mercury* 7 October 1865 page 6 column 4
182 Ibid. 23 December 1865 page 6 column 5

183 *Berkshire Chronicle* 9 January 1869 page 2 columns 2 to 3
184 *Reading Mercury* 29 September 1883 page 5 column 3
185 Ibid. 9 February 1884 page 5 column 4
186 *Berkshire Chronicle* 6 June 1885 page 8 column 4
187 *Reading Mercury* 16 October 1886 page 2 column 5 and 9 October 1886 page 5 column 3. Also, Berkshire Record Office reference R/AC1/2/10 *Reading Council Minutes 1882–1886, report of the Borough Extension and Improvement Committee of 29 May 1885*, presented to the Council meeting of 4 June 1885
188 *Reading Mercury* 13 November 1886 page 5 column 2.
189 Ibid. 16 April 1887 page 6 column 6
190 Ibid. 23 April 1887 page 5 column 2 and *Berkshire Chronicle* 30 April 1887 page 5 column 6
191 *Reading Mercury* 21 May 1887 page 5 column 2 and 24 December 1887 page 2 column 5
192 *Berkshire Chronicle* 30 June 1888 page 5 column 5
193 Ibid. 7 November 1891 page 6 column 1. The newspaper report actually stated that the minutes were of the meeting of the '28th day of October 1881', but that was a misprint.
194 Corley pages xiv–xv and 17. There is a Blue Plaque on 119/121 London Street, commemorating the site of the original biscuit bakery, although the date on the plaque is incorrect.
195 *Reading Mercury* 7 March 1857 page 5 column 6. Huntley died on 3 March 1857.
196 huntleyandpalmers.org.uk [Accessed November 2017]
197 *Reading Mercury* 16 November 1850 page 3 column 2
198 Ibid. 10 November 1883 page 5 column 5
199 Ibid. 14 November 1857 page 2 columns 3 and 6
200 Ibid. 8 January 1859 page 3 column 4
201 Ibid. 18 May 1878 page 5 columns 4 and 5; 7 February 1885 page 5 column 4
202 *Berkshire Chronicle* 21 August 1897 page 5 column 2
203 Ibid. 7 November 1891 page 6 column 3
204 *Berkshire Chronicle* 7 November 1891 page 6. Also see Corley 1972 pages 146–147
205 *Berkshire Chronicle* 21 August 1897 page 5
206 Corley 1972 page 146
207 'Petition calling for George Palmer statue to come back to Reading town centre gathering pace' in getreading.co.uk, by Hugh Fort, 21 May 2017 [Accessed November 2017]
208 *Reading Mercury* 7 January 1893 page 5 column 5
209 Corley 1972 pages 31, and 70–71. In the *Morning Post* 31 December 1856 page 7 column 1 William Isaac Palmer, as a witness in a legal case, described some actions he took at Huntley & Palmer in December 1855.
210 Corley pages 70–71
211 *Reading Mercury* 7 January 1893 page 5 column 5
212 Ibid. 21 August 1786 page 3 column 3

213 *Berkshire Chronicle* 10 June 1876 page 2. There is a shield in the Waterhouse Room in the Town Hall with inscription: 'These Municipal Buildings were opened on the 6 June 1876. Charles Smith Mayor 1874–6, R. C. Dryland Town Clerk'.
214 *Berkshire Chronicle* 10 October 1874 page 8 column 4
215 Ibid. 12 May 1877 page 4 column 3
216 *Reading Mercury* 3 June 1882 page 2
217 Ibid. 23 October 1897 page 2 column 1
218 Ibid. 7 January 1893 page 5 column 5
219 *Berkshire Chronicle* 8 April 1893 page 6 column 2
220 *Reading Mercury* 6 July 1895 page 5 column 5
221 Ibid. 23 October 1897 page 2 column 2
222 *Reading Observer* 31 July 1897 page 5 column 2
223 *Berkshire Chronicle* 31 July 1897 page 5 column 2
224 *Reading Mercury* 24 August 1861 page 6 column 6
225 Ibid. 27 July 1861 page 5 column 2. The total cost was correctly given at the opening of the hall – see next note for reference.
226 Ibid. 31 August 1861 page 6 column 1
227 *Berkshire Chronicle* 20 August 1887 page 2 column 3
228 Ibid. 30 June 1900 page 2 columns 3 and 4
229 Corley 1991–1993 pages 135–136
230 A. B. Cheales, *Martin Hope Sutton of Reading*, quoted in Earley Local History Group page 6
231 Corley 1991–1993 page 137
232 *Reading Mercury* 3 December 1832 page 3 column 5
233 *Berkshire Chronicle* 21 December 1833 page 2 columns 5 and 6; also 10 May 1834 page 1 column 2
234 Corley 1991–1993 page 139
235 *Reading Mercury* 30 June 1838 page 3 column 3
236 Corley 1991–1993 page 141
237 Ibid. page 142
238 Earley Local History Group pages 101–104
239 *Berkshire Chronicle* 10 February 1844 page 3 column 6
240 *Reading Mercury* 5 December 1846 page 3 column 6 'On the 1st inst., deeply lamented, Charlotte the beloved wife of Mr Martin Sutton, nurseryman, Reading, after many months illness, which she bore with Christian patience and resignation.'
241 *Berkshire Chronicle* 30 May 1857 page 1 column 2
242 *Reading Mercury* 20 December 1890 page 2 column 6
243 Ibid. 12 October 1901 page 2 column 1
244 Summers pages 138–143
245 Earley Local History Group *op. cit.* page 221
246 *Reading Mercury* 12 October 1901 page 2 column 1
247 Ibid. page 7 column 5
248 *Reading Mercury* 31 May 1902 page 7 column 5
249 Ibid. 29 November page 8 column 1

250 Ibid. 6 December 1902 page 2 column 5
251 historicengland.org.uk [Accessed February 2018]. List Entry Number 1113589
252 *Reading Mercury* 21 June 1902 page 2 column 3
253 *Berkshire Chronicle* 22 March 1902 page 2 column 4
254 Article by S.C. Hutchinson, quoted in victorianweb.org [Accessed February 2018].
255 *Berkshire Chronicle* 28 June 1902 page 2 column 4
256 *St James's Gazette* 24 June 1902 page 11 column 1; *Pall Mall Gazette* 24 June 1902 page 7 column 2 (Special Edition)
257 *Berkshire Chronicle* 28 June 1902 page 9 column 3
258 *Reading Mercury* 29 November 1902 page 7 column 5
259 *Berkshire Chronicle* 4 October 1902 page 3 column 4
260 *Reading Observer* 4 December 1902 page 1 column 7
261 Ibid. page 2 column 1
262 Earley Local History Group pages 223–226. Also see Alexander page 186
263 *Reading Mercury* 6 December 1902 page 2 column 4
264 J.J. Cooper page 75, Naxton page 47, *Oxford University & City Herald* 2 April 1836 page 3 column 3, and for Martha's death, *Ipswich Journal* 3 February 1781 page 1 column 3
265 *Reading Mercury* 11 April 1836 page 3 column 3
266 Ibid. 3 June 1782 page 3 column 2
267 *Bath Chronicle and Weekly Gazette* 13 June 1816 page 3 column 2. The *Reading Mercury* 10 June 1816 page 3 column 1 also noted her passing, stating that she was deeply and universally lamented, and 'unable to do justice to her character, we shall leave it to be appreciated by those who knew her excellence in every relation of life and in every Christian virtue.'
268 Naxton page 47
269 Ibid. pages 50, 58; Doran page 185
270 Darter page 19
271 Naxton pages 52 and 56. Just five years later, according to Doran page 197, the number of boys had dropped again to 40 under Dr Valpy's son Francis, his successor. Naxton page 57 states there were just 30 in 1840.
272 There are several sources that perpetuate the myth. One source will be sufficient here: Edgar Cardew Marchant's entry for Richard Valpy in the *Dictionary of National Biography 1885–1900* Volume 58, available online at wikisource.org [accessed July 2018]
273 Bockett's book is available to read online at books.google.co.uk [Accessed July 2018]
274 Many sources quote the date of publication of the *Delectus* as 1815, but this was the date of the enlarged Second Edition. For the first edition date see, for example, *Morning Post* 29 January 1813 page 2 column 3
275 Quoted in the article on Richard Valpy in Wikipedia.org [Accessed July 2018]
276 *London Evening Standard* 30 March 1836 page 4 column 6
277 historicengland.org.uke [Accessed July 2018]. List Entry Number 1389207
278 *Berkshire Chronicle* 8 December 1838 page 3 column 2

279 *Reading Mercury* 8 December 1838 page 3 column 3; *Berkshire Chronicle* 15 December 1838 page 3 column 3
280 The Latin inscription is given both in the original and in translation in Kruschwitz pages 55–56.
281 *Reading Mercury* 4 May 1878 page 6 column
282 *Reading Observer* 8 March 1902 page 2 column 7
283 *Berkshire Chronicle* 24 September 1904 page 5 column 5
284 See the chapter by Cecil Slade in Petyt pages 1–30
285 Williams & Martin (Ed.) pages 140 and 146
286 Yorke page 8
287 Quoted in Hurry 1901 page 1, from William of Malmesbury's *Gesta Regum Anglorum*, written not long after the founding of the Abbey.
288 The first source I can find with this idea is in Phillips page 21. I would be grateful to hear of any earlier sources.
289 The charter is quoted in Hurry 1901 page 151. Also see Albury page 68
290 Hurry 1906 page 4
291 Kemp page 102
292 Ibid. page 105
293 The various posts undertaken by the Rev Nicholas Hurry are given in the Surman Index Online, at surman.english.qmul.ac.uk [Accessed July 2018]
294 The Medical Directory for 1890 (J & A Churchill, London 1890) pages 707–708
295 Liverpool, England, Crew Lists 1861–1919 and New South Wales, Australia, Unassisted Passenger Lists 1826–1922, both online at ancestry.co.uk [Accessed July 2018]
296 The Medical Directory for 1890 (J & A Churchill, London 1890) page 707
297 Hurry 1909 pages 1, 145, 148 and 151
298 This list is not exhaustive. The pages of the Reading newspapers abound with the name of Dr Hurry from 1885.
299 The story of the provision of the West End Library has been well told by Cliffe – see Bibliography.
300 *Berkshire Chronicle* 20 January 1906 page 8 column 3
301 Ibid. 29 April 1908 page 7 columns 1 and 2
302 *Reading Observer* 6 March 1909 page 2 column 3 and *Berkshire Chronicle* 6 March 1909 page 9 column 4
303 *Manchester Courier* and *Lancashire General Advertiser* 3 May 1909 page 6 column 1
304 *Northern Whig* 10 May 1909 page 7 column 3
305 *Votes for Women* 25 June 1909 page 850 column 2
306 *Berkshire Chronicle* 19 June 1909 page 7 column 3
307 *Reading Mercury* 15 July 1911 page 2 columns 4 and 5
308 *Reading Observer* 7 December 1912 page 2 column 7
309 Ibid. 14 June 1913 page 3 column 4 and 21 June 1913 page 6 columns 1 and 2
310 See ww2.readingmuseum.org.uk for detail on the Abbey Paintings [Accessed July 2018]
311 *Reading Observer* 25 June 1921 page 1 columns 1 to 3
312 *Windsor and Eton Express* 27 August 1910 page 2 column 5

313 *Reading Observer* 2 July 1910 page 2 column 6
314 Smith page 4
315 Ibid. page 5
316 Ibid. page 33
317 Ibid. pages 35 and 40
318 Ibid. page 12
319 Haultain page 17
320 *Berkshire Chronicle* 6 August 1842 page 4 column 5
321 Wallace pages 5 and 6; see also Foster 1893 page 30
322 Foster 1885 page 432
323 Smith page 75
324 J.J. Cooper page 39. The *Reading Mercury* 31 March 1866 page 5 column 1 states the reason that Smith wished to 'devote his energies ... to the historical works which he has on hand'.
325 *Berkshire Chronicle* 12 October 1867 page 6 columns 1 and 2
326 Ibid. 30 November 1867 page 7 column 3
327 J.J. Cooper page 39
328 Wallace page 40
329 Smith page 450
330 *The Sphere* 11 May 1907 page 12 column 1
331 *Macmillan's Magazine* Volume XI (November 1864–April 1865) (Macmillan & Co, Cambridge 1865) page 300
332 Wilson & Fiske (Ed.) page 565
333 *Manchester Courier and Lancashire General Advertiser* 15 June 1882 page 8 column 6
334 *Reading Observer* 9 June 1910 page 3 column 3
335 Ibid. 11 June 1910 page 5 column 5
336 Quoted in Wallace page 287
337 *Reading Observer* 20 August 1910 page 5 column 7
338 Ibid. 3 February 1912 page 2 column 3
339 Ibid. 10 September 1921 page 5 column 6
340 Ibid. 2 April 1921 page 5 column 4
341 Ibid. 26 March 1921 page 1 column 5
342 Ibid. 11 February 1922 page 3 column 4
343 Ibid. 8 December 1922 page 2 column 4. Also see *Reading Mercury* 25 April 1931 page 10 columns 4 and 5
344 *Reading Observer* 10 November 1922 page 8 column 2
345 *Reading Mercury* 25 April 1931 page 10 column 4
346 *Reading Standard* 5 March 1932 page 13 column 3
347 Ibid. 4 June 1932 page 11 column 3
348 Ibid. 30 July 1932 page 6 columns 1 to 3; also see the photographs in that issue on page 7. *Reading Mercury* 30 July 1932 page 8 columns 1 and 2
349 *The London Gazette* 1 October 1915 page 9641 column 2. This mistakenly calls Potts Alfred, which is corrected in the Supplement to the edition on 18 October 1915 page 10249 column 1. It is quoted on the information board by the Berkshire Yeomanry Memorial, The Forbury. Also see, for example, *Reading Observer* 9 October 1915 page 3 column 3

350 *Reading Mercury* 18 December 1915 page 7 column 4
351 getreading.co.uk 26 April 2010, article by David Millward 'Burma Star tribute to war veterans' [Accessed April 2018]
352 Parkes, Jerrome & Cooper pages 11 to 18
353 Cooper & Parkes
354 *Evening Post* 8 May 1990 page 5. Article by Paul Pickett
355 Parkes, Jerrome & Cooper page 8
356 *Reading Chronicle* 16 May 2015 at readingchronicle.co.uk [Accessed October 2017]
357 Parkes, Jerrome & Cooper, available online at international-brigades.org.uk [Accessed October 2017]
358 Ibid. page 10

Afterword

Past Reading citizens, and especially those of the 19th century, have done a good job in keeping the stories they considered to be important before our notice through the memorials they took the trouble to create.

What will modern Reading enable future generations to be reminded of? The town does have some memorials from the last 25 years. Two examples would be the plaque on Broad Street recording the completion of its pedestrianisation in May 1994, and the 2017 Blue Plaque on Talbot House, Castle Street, commemorating Phoebe Cusden MBE, former Mayor of Reading and co-founder of the Reading Dusseldorf Association.

Perhaps, however, we do not have many philanthropists of the same prominence as Edward Simeon or Jamieson B. Hurry, or many citizens as notable as Dr Valpy or Goldwin Smith. Certainly, the town's industries do not dominate the employment market as did Sutton & Sons and Huntley & Palmers. Nevertheless, let us hope that Reading will continue its tradition of making every effort to commemorate significant people and events so that the generations to come will be able to look back and remember what was important in our time.

Bibliography

Fred W. Albury, 'Reading Abbey, Its History and Architecture' in *Transactions of the Berkshire Archaeological & Architectural Society* (J.J. Beecroft, Reading 1881)

Alan Alexander, *Borough Government and Politics: Reading 1835–1985* (George Allen & Unwin, London 1985)

W. E. M. Blandy, *A History of the Reading Municipal Charities* (Greenslade & Co., Reading 1962)

Rev B. B. Bockett, *Our School: or Scraps and Scrapes in Schoolboy Life by Oliver Oldfellow M.A. Oxon* (John Wesley & Co, London 1857)

Rev William Carus, M.A., *The Life of the Rev. Charles Simeon, M.A.* (Hatchard & Son, London 1847)

W. M. Childs, *The Town of Reading during the Early Part of the Nineteenth Century* (Reading 1910)

David Cliffe, *Roots and Branches* (Two Rivers Press, Reading 2007)

Rev Charles Coates, *The History and Antiquities of Reading* (J. Nichols & Son, London 1802)

John James Cooper, *Some Worthies of Reading* (The Swarthmore Press, London 1923)

Mike Cooper and Ray Parkes, *We Cannot Park on Both Sides* (Reading International Brigades Memorial Committee 2000)

T. A. B. Corley, *Quaker Enterprise in Biscuits: Huntley and Palmers of Reading, 1822–1972* (Hutchinson, London 1972)

T. A. B. Corley, 'The Making of a Berkshire Entrepreneur: Martin Hope Sutton of Reading: 1815–40' (*Berkshire Archaeological Journal*, Volume 74, 1991–1993)

Rev G. P. Crawfurd, Curate of St Mary's, Reading, 'Vachell, of Coley, Reading' (*The Quarterly Journal of the Berks Archaeological and Architectural Society*, Volume III Reading 1893)

W. S. Darter, *Reminiscences of Reading, by an Octogenarian* (Reading 1890)

P. H. Ditchfield (Ed.), *Reading Seventy Years Ago* (John Read, Reading 1887)

John Doran, *The History and Antiquities of the Town and Borough of Reading in Berkshire* (Samuel Reader, Reading 1835)

Earley Local History Group, *Suttons Seeds: A History 1806–2006* (2006)

Rev J. Field, *The Advantages of the Separate System of Imprisonment as Established in the New County Gaol at Reading* Volume 1 (Longmans, London 1848)

Joseph Foster, *Men-At-The-Bar* (Hazell, Watson & Viney, London 1885)

Joseph Foster, *Oxford Men and Their Colleges* (James Parker & Co., Oxford and London 1893)

Rev J. M. Guilding (Ed.), *Reading Records: Diary of the Corporation* Volume 3 (1630–1640) (James Parker & Co., London 1896)

Rupert Gunnis, *A Biographical Dictionary of Sculptors in Britain 1660-1851* (Abbey Library, London 1968) (Revised Edition)

Arnold Haultain, *Goldwin Smith, His Life and Opinions* (T. Werner Laurie Ltd, London 1913)

Michael Hinton, *A History of the Town of Reading* (Harrap, London 1954)

Jamieson B. Hurry, *Reading Abbey* (Elliot Stock, London 1901)

Jamieson B. Hurry, *The Rise and Fall of Reading Abbey* (Elliot Stock, London 1906)

Jamieson B. Hurry, *A History of the Reading Pathological Society* (Bale & Danielsson, London 1909)

Jamieson B. Hurry, 'Hugh II., Eighth Abbot of Reading' (*The Berks, Bucks & Oxon Archaeological Journal*, Volume 22 No. 4 January 1917)

Stuart Hylton, *Reading A Pictorial History* (Phillimore & Co, Chichester 1994)

Brian Kemp (Ed.), *Reading Abbey Records a new miscellany* (Berkshire Record Society Volume 25 2018)

Rev Charles Kerry, *A History of the Municipal Church of St Lawrence, Reading* (Reading 1883)

Peter Kruschwitz, *The Writing on the Wall: Reading's Latin Inscriptions* (Two Rivers Press, Reading 2015)

John Man, *The Stranger in Reading in a Series of Letters from a Traveller to his Friend in London* (Snare & Man, Reading 1810)

John Man, *The History and Antiquities, Ancient and Modern, of the Borough of Reading* (Snare & Man, Reading 1816)

Michael Naxton, *The History of Reading School* (1986)

John Nixon, *The Gentlemen Danes* (1993)

Leslie North, *Royal Reading's Colourful Past* (Cressrelles, Peppard Common 1979)

Ray Parkes, Keith Jerrome & Mike Cooper, *Defended Democracy: Reading's International Brigades Memorial* (Reading International Brigades Memorial Trust 2015)

Malcolm Petyt (Ed.), *The Growth of Reading* (Alan Sutton, Stroud 1993)

Daphne Phillips, *The Story of Reading* (Countryside Books, Newbury 1980)

Hugo Ryberg, *A List of Inhabitants of The Danish Westindian Islands from 1650 – ca.1825* (Copenhagen 1945)

Goldwin Smith, *Reminiscences* (Macmillan, New York 1910)

Adam Sowan, *A Mark of Affection: The Soane Obelisk in Reading* (Two Rivers Press, Reading 2007)

Adam Sowan, *All Change at Reading* (Two Rivers Press, Reading 2013)

Richard J. Stacpoole-Ryding, *Maiwand: The Last Stand of the 66th (Berkshire) Regiment in Afghanistan, 1880* (The History Press, Stroud 2008)

Malcolm Summers, *History of Greyfriars Church, Reading* (Downs Way Publishing, Reading 2013)

Elisabeth Wallace, *Goldwin Smith, Victorian Liberal* (University of Toronto Press 1957)

Ann Williams & G.H. Martin, *Domesday Book: A Complete Translation* (Penguin, London 2002)

James Grant Wilson & John Fiske (Ed.), *Appleton's Cyclopaedia of American Biography* Volume 5 (D. Appleton & Co., New York 1888)

Alan Windsor, 'The Simeon Monument in Reading by Sir John Soane', in Bold and Chaney (Eds), *English Architecture Public and Private* (The Hambledon Press, London 1993)

Barbara Yorke, *Kings and Kingdoms of Early Anglo-Saxon England* (Routledge, London 2002)

Index

66th (Berkshire) Regiment 44–50
A'Larder almshouses 4, 5, 64
A'Larder, John 4
Abbey *also see* Reading Abbey
Abbey abbot's lodge 9
Abbey gates 9 *also see* Compter Gate
Abbey gateway, inner 9, 29, 115
Abbey Hospitium 9, 76, 93, 95
Abbey mill 9
Abbey Quarter 61, 118
Abbey Plummery Wall 9
Abbey ruins 1, 31, 34, 35, 70, 104
Abbey School 115
Abbey Square 9
Abbot Hugh I (de Boves) 103
Abbot Hugh II 9
Abbot Hugh Cook Faringdon 103
Abbotsbrook 100, 101
Abbots Walk 118
Afghanistan 44, 47
Albion FC 72
Alexandra, Queen 87
Allen, Dr H. P. 104
Almshouses 2, 4–8, 20, 64, 70
Ament, Conrad 25
America 27, 32, 108
   also see United States
Amersham Hall School 102
Ames, Anne 114
Ancient Order of Shepherds 72
Andrewes, Charles J. 6
Andrewes, Edward 2
Annesley, Francis 31
Aragon 118
Art Gallery 75, 77, 78, 93, 95, 97, 104
Austen, Jane 109
Austwick, Lancelot 15, 16, 21

Baker, William 15
Ball, Rev John 6, 7, 42
Ball, Charles 6

Ball, William 118
Bank of England 13, 15
Bardsey 63
Bath 105
Bath Road 63, 75
Battle 2
Battle Library 101
Bayeux Tapestry (copy) 78
Bedford Road 21
Belgium 48
Bell, Julian 117
Benwell, Mary 93
Benyon, James Herbert 49, 113
Benyon, Richard 58
Berkshire Rifle Volunteer Corps 47
Berkshire Society of Architects 111
Binfield, Sarah 27
Binyon, Robert Laurence 114
Birch, T. F. 7
Birrell, Rt Hon Augustine 102, 103
Biscuit Factory Cricket Club 72
Blagrave, Eliza 107
Blagrave Estate 65
Blagrave, John 33, 107
Blagrave, J. H. 97
Blagrave, John (c1561–1611) 11
Blagrave Piazza 11, 41, 43
Blagrave Street 57, 58, 61, 75, 77, 91, 97
Blake, T. H. 58
Blake's Bridge 9
Bland, Horatio 77
Bland Garland, Thomas 76
Blandy, H. B. 7, 77, 97
Blandy, John Jackson 6, 7, 37, 42
Blandy, W. 6, 7
Blandy, W. E. M. 20
Blandy, W. F. 66
Blue Coat School 113
Boar's Head 37, 38
Bockett, Rev B. B. 96

Bodenheffs, Hans 27
Bolland, Mr Baron 96
Boulton, Harriet Elizabeth Mann
  108, 109
Bournemouth 100
Boyd, Ann Shaw Jamieson 100
Boyd, John 100
Braag, Cecilia 23
Braag, Dominicus 23
Braag , Laurenthes 23-27
Braag, Paul 23
Braag Winther, Birgith 27
Brain, John A. 70
Brandt, Markus 25
Breton, Eliza 105
Bridge Street 48
Brighton 77
Brimpton 48
Brinkworth 33
Bristol 75, 102
Broad Street 6, 33, 64, 69, 70, 72, 73, 131
Brock Barracks 111
Brooke, Alice 2
Brown, Messrs W. & J.T. 97
Brunete 117
Buckingham Palace 88, 115
Bull, Alfred Holland 87, 90
Bullock, Rev H.A. 114
Burghfield 76
Burrows, George Scott Reynolds
  44, 46
Bury St Edmund's School 93
Butler, Charles J. 6

Calcot Park 107
Calcutta 47
Callas, Sons & May 86
Cambridge 102
Cambridge, 2nd Duke of 58-60
Cambridge, Holy Trinity Church 13
Cambridge, St John's College 100
Canada 108-110
Carnegie, Andrew 101

Carrit, Anthony 117
Casa de Gampo 118
Castle 31
Castle Inn 2
Castle Street 2, 4, 6, 7, 8, 61, 63-65, 70, 81, 100, 101, 131
Catley *see* Collier
Cava Gioia Quarry 57
Caversham 4, 34, 76, 93, 101, 102
Caversham Road 86
Caversham Urban District Council 101
Chain Lane *see* Chain Street
Chain Street 4, 5
Charity Commissioners 4, 5, 20, 64
Charles I, charter of 30
Chatham 27
Chaucer 79
Christian, Prince 87, 91, 92
Christiansted 23
Church of England 67, 115
Church Street 73
Cintra Lodge 85
Civic Offices 117, 118
Civil War 9, 31 *also see* Spanish
Clayton & Bell, Messrs 47
Coates, Rev Charles 4
Colebrook, William Merrill 101
Coley 2, 49
Coley Park/estate 2
Coley Street 4, 8
Collier & Catley 113
Collier, Samuel 6
Colston Hall 102
Compter Gate 9, 11, 12
Compter House 11, 43
Compter Prison 9, 11, 12
Consolidated Church Almshouse Charities 4-7, 65
Consolidated General Almshouse Charities 4-7, 64, 65
Cooper, John James 97, 108, 110
Cooper, L. 6
Cooper, Sarah Selina 27
Copenhagen 23, 24

Corn Exchange 15, 20, 92
Cornelius, Martha 93
Cornell University 108, 110
Corporation 2, 4, 6, 11, 12, 13, 15, 16, 18–20, 26, 29–33, 39, 49, 51, 53, 54, 69, 70, 76, 77, 91, 93, 95, 97, 110
Counter *see* Compter
Cowper 109
Cox & Co., Messrs 48
Cox, F. A. 110
Craig's Court 48
Craig, Thora 117
Crapp, F. J. 47
Cromwell 108
Crown Street 65
Cusden, Phoebe MBE 131
Cust, Rev Arthur P. Purey 7, 63

Dahlerup, Hans Birch 27
Dale, T. Lawrence 111
Danish West Indies 23
Darter, W. S. 6
Day, Henry 69, 78, 90
Dell, Barton 75
Denmark 23, 24
Dickens, Charles 79
Ditchfield, Rev P. H. 104
Domesday Book 99
Doran, John 4
Dover 24
Dunkinfield, Katherine 107
Dunkinfield, Sir Nathaniel 107
Dunn, B. 65
Dymore Brown, James 5

Earley 84
East Reading FC 72
Edgehill Street 115
Edison, Thomas 79
Edward VII 84, 87, 88, 90–92, 108
  also see Wales, Edward, Prince of
Edward the Confessor 99
Egypt 47

Elberton 75
Elizabeth I, charter of 11, 29, 30
Elizabeth I, Queen 11
England 23, 24, 41, 48, 99, 100, 103
Erleigh Court 101
Erleigh Road 97
Essex 100
Eton 105, 107
Evans, Jane 69, 75
Exall, W. 6

Ferguson, William 77, 78
Fielder, Rt Rev John 63
Fitt's Monumental Works 79
Forbury 9, 13, 29–34, 39, 41, 49, 58, 59, 70, 72, 83, 86, 95, 97, 113, 115, 117
Forbury Gardens 9, 29, 44, 48, 49, 90, 99, 102, 115, 117, 118
Forbury Hill 29–31, 33–35, 115
Forbury Road 9
Foresters' Society 72, 90
Fosbery, Rev T. V. 6, 7
Fowler, George C. 48
Foxhill House 76
Fox Talbot, William Henry 27
Frame, William 110
Francis, Archibald 118
Fredericksen, Knud 25, 27
Free Library 70, 76–78, 101, 110
Friar Street 16, 37, 38, 50, 51, 57, 58, 105, 107, 109
Friars Place 79
Frith, W. S. 104
Frome 71

Galbraith, James 44
Gallipoli 115
Garry, Canon N. T. 66
Gaskell, Lois 115
George III 26
George V 115
George Hotel 1
George, Mrs 60

Germany 48, 117
Girishk 44, 49
Gloucestershire 75
Goldwin, Thomas 105
Goring 15
Grange 108, 109
Great Garston 2
Greathead, Thomas 81
Great Western Railway 37–39, 58, 84, 85, 92
Green School 6
Greyfriars Church 1, 81, 83, 86
Greyfriars Road 81
Greyfriars, Vicar of 85, 86
Greyfriars Vicarage 16
Grissell, Thomas 37
Guildford 93
Guildhall 20 *also see* Town Hall
Guilding, Rev J. M. 58
Gunston, E. Leslie 113

Hall, John 4
Hall, John, almshouses 4, 5
Halversen, Erick 25
Handel 76
Harrinson, Isaac 54, 63, 65–67, 100
Harris T. 7
Harris W. 7
Harrison, Bernard 4, 5
Harrison, Bernard, almshouses 4–6
Hasteed, John 11
Hawkes, F. & Sons 83
Heelas, Daniel 69
Helmand River 44
Henley Park 87, 91
Henry I, Beauclerc, King 79, 99–104
Hewett, R. 6
Highbridge House 12
Hiley, Haviland 93
Hill, Arthur 49, 54, 57, 60, 78, 101
Hill, Elizabeth 11
Hill, Gertrude 101
Hillfields 76
Holborn 41

Hole, the 11
Holmes, Sherlock 50
Holy Brook 6–9
Homer 79
Horton 2
Hosier Street 63
Hounslow, John Wells 63
Howard, John 12
Howell, William Roland 77, 111
Hospitium *see* Abbey
Huntley & Palmer 69, 75
Huntley & Palmers 58, 69, 75, 77, 91, 131
Huntley Joseph (Jun.) 75
Huntley, Joseph (Sen.) 81
Huntley, Thomas 69, 75
Hurry, Dr Jamieson Boyd 99–104, 110
Hurry, Rev Nicholas 100
Imperial and Colonial Institute 57

India 44, 47, 60, 92
Indonesia 32
Inner Distribution Road 8
Italy 48, 57, 117
Ithaca 108

Jamieson, Ann 100
Jarama 118
Java, Isle of 27
Jersey 93
Johnsen, Torvel 25
Jones, A. F. 21
Jones, Tony 118
Jorgensen, Anthony 25

Kandahar 44, 46, 49, 50
Kendrick, William 4
Kendrick, William, almshouses 4–6
Kennet, River 9, 34, 99
Kensal Green Cemetery 96
Kensington 76, 78, 95, 96
Khan, Ayub 44, 46, 47
Khan, Sher Ali 44

King's College School 96
King's Meadows 70
King Street 1, 81, 83, 84
King's Road 9, 58, 70, 72
Knollys, Francis, Sir 11
Knollys, Francis, Sir (younger) 2
Knollys, Lettice 2
Knollys Transept 11

Lainson, Thomas 77
Lane, Sarah 2
Lawley, William 11
Leche, John *see* A'Larder
Leeds 102
Lefevre, Charles Shaw 17, 18
Lemeke, Hans Jurgen 25
Lewis, Herbert 24, 26
Lincoln, Abraham 109
Lincoln's Inn 107
Lindsey, Jack 118
Little Garston 2
Liverpool 41, 75, 100, 102, 115
Lockey, Maureen 117
Lodge, J. 7
London 9, 13, 26, 37, 39, 41, 48, 57, 72, 76, 81, 88, 92, 96, 100, 102, 107
London Road 79, 84
London Street 69, 75, 81
London University 111
London Zoo 48
Longley, J.W. 109
Long Sutton 69

Macartney, Mervyn L. 111
Maiwand 44, 46–50, 57–59, 70, 113, 114
Major, Rev Dr 96
Malmund Pass 44
Man, John 4, 13, 20, 21, 29
Market Place 11, 12, 13, 15, 16, 18, 20, 21, 41, 48, 58, 84, 108
Marks & Spencer 58
Marlstone House 69, 91

Marsh & Deane 81
May & Hurry 100
May, Ellen 63
May, George (older) 63, 101
May, George (younger) 100, 101
May, William Charles 79
Melly, Charles Pierre 41
Merewether, Sgt. 96
Middle Row 63–65, 70
Middleton, George 117, 118
Miller, R.P. 6
Minster Street 72, 84
Moller, Christiane 23
Monck, John Berkeley 6, 7, 17, 18, 27
Monck, John Bligh 63, 64
Monkton Farleigh 105
Moon, Jimmy, 117
Morris 86
Morris, E. 7
Morris, T. 6, 7
Mortimer 107, 108
Murdoch, C.T. 54
Murphy, Tom 115

Nansen, Fridtjof 79
Napoleon 23, 24, 81
National Railway Museum 39
Natural History Museum 76
Neuchâtel 100
New South Wales 100
Newton, William 9
New York 97, 108
Nixon, John 27
Nixon, Samuel 96
Normandy 93
Northamptonshire 2
Norway 27

Oddfellows 72, 90
Old Street 4 *also see* St Mary's Butts
Oliver, John 115
Opie 96
Osborne House 84, 87
Osler, Sir William 103

Owen, Thomas 19
Oxford 91
Oxford, Diocese of 63, 66, 111
Oxford Road 111
Oxford, University 93, 96, 103–105, 107, 109

Paddington 91
Pain, James 72
Palmer *also see* Huntley & Palmer(s)
Palmer, George 5, 6, 50, 69–73, 75, 77–79, 91
Palmer, George, Mrs 72
Palmer, George William 91
Palmer, Mary, Mrs Samuel 75, 77
Palmer Memorial Hall, W.I. 79, 80
Palmer Park 69, 72, 73
Palmer Samuel 69, 75, 77, 78, 80
Palmer Samuel Ernest 77, 81
Palmer William Isaac 5, 41, 69, 75–80
Parents' National Education Union 100
Parkhurst 48
Parkes, Ray 117–119
Parry, Albert W. 51, 57
Peck, Mr 43
Peyman, General 24
Phelps, Rev W.W. 38
Pimlico 49
Pinckneys Meadow 2
Pitt 108
Ponsonby, Sir Henry 61
Potts, Trooper Fred VC 114, 115
Poulsen, Hans 27
Poulton, Charles 76
Poulton & Woodman 41
Pountney, W.H. 58
Primrose, General 47, 49
Pulsometer Engineering Works 115
Puxley, James 115
Pym 108
Pugh, Fred 27
Queen Anne's School 102

Queen Victoria Institute 20, 100
Queen's Hotel 60

Radcliffe, Tom 118
Railway Heritage Committee 39
Ravenscroft, Son & Morris 86
Ravenscroft, William 97, 102–104
Reading & District Burma Star Association 115
Reading & District Licensed Trade 88
Reading Abbey 4, 9, 11, 29, 30, 79, 99–104 *also see* Abbey
Reading Almshouse Charity 7
Reading Arms (public house) 12
Reading Athletics Club 72
Reading Borough Council 21, 39, 43, 78, 117, 118
Reading Cemetery Co. 100
Reading Central Library 9, 30
Reading Civic Society 27
Reading Dispensary Trust 5, 100
Reading Dusseldorf Association 131
Reading FC 72
Reading Friendly Society 72, 90
Reading Gaol 10, 32
Reading Gas Co. 100
Reading Horticultural Society 83
Reading Local Board of Health 41
Reading Literary and Scientific Society 100
Reading Museum 7, 27, 70, 76–78, 101, 104, 117
Reading Natural History Society 100
Reading Orpheus Society 73
Reading Pathological Society 67, 100
Reading Philharmonic Society 67, 73
Reading Rowing Club 72
Reading School 29, 31, 76, 93, 95–97
Reading Station 37–39 *also see* Great Western Railway
Reading Temperance Society 79
Reading University 76, 117
Ready, J.T. 48
Red Cross Society 111

Regent Inns plc 39
Riiberg, Sivert 27
Rixon, F.G. 39
Roberts, Lord 46
Roche Abbey 96
Rogers, Thomas 41, 42, 76
Routh, Martin 107
Rowley Road 115
Royal Berkshire Regiment 111, 113, 114 *also see* 66th (Berkshire) Regiment
Royal Berkshire Volunteers 58, 72
Royal Berkshire Yeomanry 58, 71, 91, 115
Royal Victoria Studios 61
Russell, Charles 37
Russell, John 110

St Anne's Well 101
St Bartholomew's Hospital 100
St Croix, Island of 23
St Croix Lutheran Church of 23
St Giles's Church/parish 1, 2, 4, 25, 27, 115
St Giles's Men's Society 115
St John Ambulance Association 100
St Laurence's (or Lawrence's) Church/parish 1, 2, 4, 9, 11, 16, 25, 27, 37–39, 41, 43, 72, 76, 85, 96, 108
St Laurence's curate of 38
St Laurence's vicar of 42, 58, 114
St Mary's Butts 4, 41, 51, 52, 54, 57, 63–66, 113
St Mary's Church/parish 1, 2, 4, 8, 23, 25–27, 47, 48, 51, 52, 63–66, 84
St Mary's Vicar of 7, 27, 63, 66
St Michaels' Church 63
St Sepulchre's Church 41
Sackville Street 81, 86
Sainsbury, F.G. 111, 113
Salisbury 66
Sawyer, J.W. 7
Saxton, Reg 117
Schleswig-Holstein 87, 91

Schools of Science and Art 76, 77
Scimitar Hill 115
Scott, George Gilbert 32
Scott, John 11
Sevenoaks 100
Shakespeare 96
Shenton, Canon Brian 27
Shepherd, Emma 115
Shiplake 34
Sidcot 75
Sieviers' Street *see* Silver Street
Silverthorne, Thora 117
Simeon 12
Simeon, Charles, Rev 13
Simeon, Edward 13, 15–21, 131
Simeon, Elizabeth 13
Simeon, John, Sir 13, 18
Simeon, Richard 13
Simonds, Blackall 50
Simonds, George (Blackall) 48, 50, 57, 70, 78
Simonds, H & G, Brewery 16, 48, 50
Simonds, Henry A. 6, 42
Simonds, H.J. 7
Simonds, James 65
Simonds, William Blackall 16
Silver Street 4
Singer, Messrs 71
Sisley & Goodall, Messrs 51
Smallcombe, W.A. 7
Smith, Eliza 105
Smith, Goldwin 105, 107–110, 131
Smith, Dr Richard Prichard 105, 108
Soane, John, Sir 15–17, 21
Soane Museum 16
Society of Friends' Burial Ground 73
Somerset 69
Sonning 34
Soole, Rev Seymour Henry 85, 86
Southcote Road 101
South-Eastern Railway 85
South-Western Railway 85
Southampton 93
Southampton Street 4

Soviet Union 117
Spanish Civil War 117, 118
Spicer, Rev John 29-31, 93
Spiller, Robert 16
Stallwood, Spencer Slingsby 66, 67, 79
Stanford, Eric 117
Stephen, King 101
Stevens, Harriet 34
Stevens, John 34
Stevens, Mr 31, 34
Stradishall 95, 96
Strickland, Mr 69
Suffolk 95
Suffragette 99, 102
Sutton & Sons 58, 81, 84, 87, 92, 131
Sutton, Alfred 84, 85
Sutton, Arthur Warwick 85
Sutton, John 81, 83
Sutton, John & Son 84
Sutton, Laura 85
Sutton, Martin Hope 81, 84-87, 92
Sutton, Martin John 85, 87, 89, 91, 92
Sutton, Sarah 81
Swimming Club 72
Switzerland 100
Sydenham, J.E. 66
Sydney 100

Talbot, Messrs G.W. & Son 101
Talbot House 131
Talbot Lodge Studios 61
Talfourd, Thomas Noon 96
Tambora, Mount 32
Tarrant, Chris OBE 115
Thames, River 9, 34, 99
Thames Water Co. 43
Thomas, Prof J. Harvard 111
Tilehurst 63, 107
Toronto 108, 109
Torquay 100

Town Council 11, 20, 35, 41, 51, 55, 57, 58, 61, 64, 65, 69, 76, 90, 91, 97, 101, 102
Town Hall 7, 16, 18, 31, 56, 58, 60, 61, 69, 70, 72, 73, 76-78, 83, 87, 91, 93, 95, 104
Tramway Co. 72
Trendell, Charlotte 84

Underwood, Rose 11
United States of America 97, 108, 117 *also see* America
United Yeast Company 7
University Extension College Council 100

Vachel(l) Almshouses 2-8
Vachel(l), Thomas, Sir (1560-1638) 2, 4, 5, 8
Valognes 93
Valparaiso 100
Valpy, Edward 97
Valpy, Francis 95
Valpy, Richard, Dr 31, 93, 95-97, 131
Valpy Street 75, 77, 93, 95, 97
Vansittart, H. 33
Vastern Road 9
Victoria Cross 115
Victoria Gate 113
Victoria Hall 76
Victoria, Queen 50, 51, 53-55, 57-61, 66, 70, 79, 84, 87
Vines, Anne 33
Vines, David 33
Vines, Joshua 29, 32-35

Wade, George Edward 88, 92
Wales, Edward, Prince of 84, 87, 92, 108
Walford, T.L. 6
Wali 44
Walker, A.B. & Son 115
Wallinscot. 1st Baronet *see* Simeon, Sir John

Walters, J.H. 109
Waltonian Angling Society 72
Warwick, Sophia Woodhead 85
Wanstead 100
Wantage, Lord 49
Water Works Company 42
Waterhouse, Alfred 76, 97
Watlington House 34
Watson, Dr 50
Webb, George W. 49, 51
Webb, Mr R. 83
Wells, Dr 42
Wellsteed, Mr & Mrs J.T. 115
Wellsteed, Ruth 115
Westfield 101
West End Library 101
West, George 39
West, Henry 37, 38
West Reading Library 101
West Street 79, 83
West Street Hall 79, 80
West, William 38 *also see* Henry
Westmacott 96

Westminster 17
Westminster Abbey 99
Wheble, Mr 35
Wheeler, Messrs 42, 49, 51, 67, 70, 86
White, Andrew 108
White, S, Victor 61
Whitley Hill 85
Wight, Isle of 48, 84, 87
William of Malmesbury 99
Wilton 38
Wiltshire 33, 38
Winchester, Dean of 104
Windsor Castle 84
Woodley Volunteer Troop of Cavalry 26
Woodman, William Henry 5, 7, 8, 41, 79
Working Men's Regatta 72

York 39
Yorkshire 63, 96
Young & Co, Messrs H. 49, 50

Two Rivers Press has been publishing in and about Reading since 1994.
Founded by the artist Peter Hay (1951–2003), the press continues
to delight readers, local and further afield, with its varied list
of individually designed, thought-provoking books.